RECORDMANIA

LITTLE GESTALTEN

⊕ TABLE OF CONTENTS ⊕

SMALLEST / BIGGEST

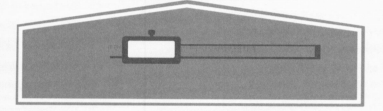

- DINOSAURS
- ANIMALS
- HUMANS
- ARCHITECTURE
- TECHNOLOGY
- ASTRONOMY
- NATURE
- SPORTS

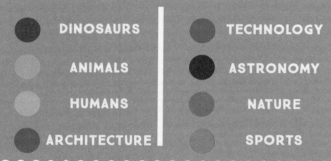

Measurements

In ancient times, the Egyptians calculated the length of an object in cubits, which is to say, in forearms. One cubit equaled the length of a person's forearm. Today, nearly all the countries in the world use the same system for measuring. They measure the size (length, height, width) of an object using an instrument (such as a height gauge, ruler, or rangefinder), and then they calculate its size either in meters, or in multiples of meters: kilometers, centimeters, decameters, etc. The exceptions? Liberia, Myanmar, the United Kingdom, and the United States all measure small objects in inches and large ones in feet.

1 EGYPTIAN CUBIT = AROUND 53 CM	1 INCH = 2.54 CM	1 FOOT = 30.48 CM

THE SMALLEST   THE BIGGEST

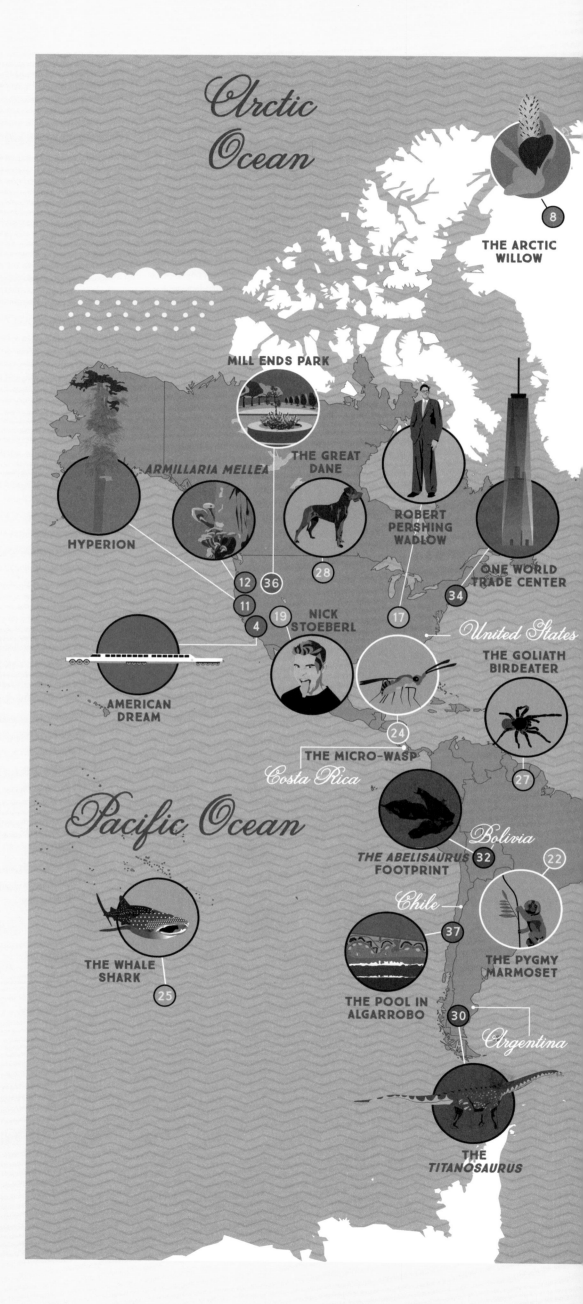

Arctic Ocean

THE ARCTIC WILLOW — 8

MILL ENDS PARK

THE GREAT DANE

ROBERT PERSHING WADLOW

ONE WORLD TRADE CENTER

ARMILLARIA MELLEA

HYPERION

12   36
11
4   19

28

17

34

NICK STOEBERL

United States

THE GOLIATH BIRDEATER

AMERICAN DREAM

24

THE MICRO-WASP

Costa Rica

Pacific Ocean

27

THE ABELISAURUS FOOTPRINT   32

Bolivia

22

Chile   37

THE PYGMY MARMOSET

THE WHALE SHARK   25

THE POOL IN ALGARROBO

30   Argentina

THE TITANOSAURUS

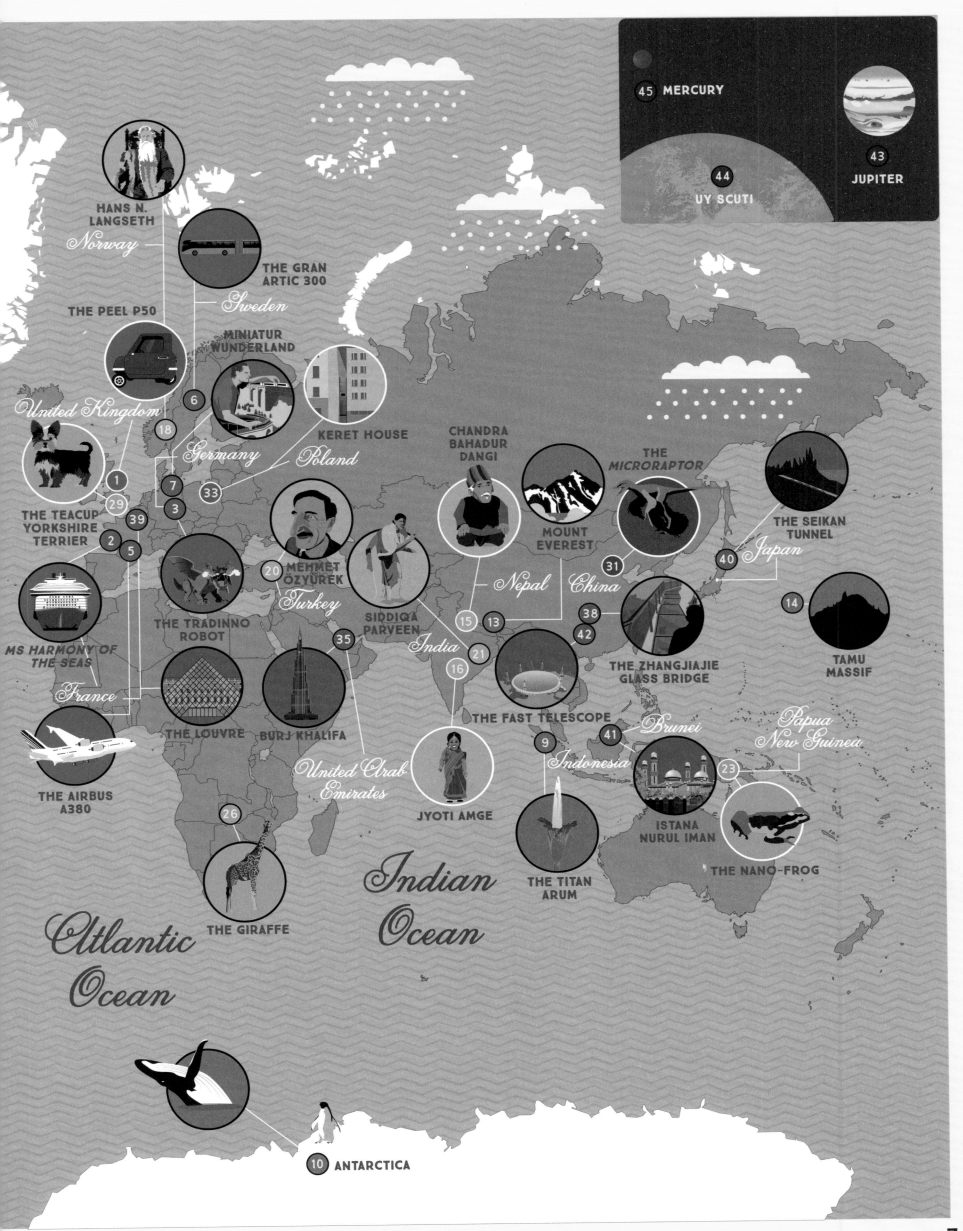

HANS N. LANGSETH
Norway

THE GRAN ARTIC 300

Sweden

THE PEEL P50

MINIATUR WUNDERLAND

United Kingdom

KERET HOUSE

Germany

Poland

CHANDRA BAHADUR DANGI

THE MICRORAPTOR

THE SEIKAN TUNNEL

THE TEACUP YORKSHIRE TERRIER

MOUNT EVEREST

Japan

MS HARMONY OF THE SEAS

MEHMET ÖZYÜREK

Turkey

SIDDIQA PARVEEN

Nepal   *China*

THE ZHANGJIAJIE GLASS BRIDGE

TAMU MASSIF

France

THE TRADINNO ROBOT

India

THE FAST TELESCOPE

THE AIRBUS A380

THE LOUVRE

BURJ KHALIFA

United Arab Emirates

JYOTI AMGE

Brunei

Papua New Guinea

Indonesia

ISTANA NURUL IMAN

THE GIRAFFE

THE TITAN ARUM

THE NANO-FROG

Indian Ocean

Atlantic Ocean

ANTARCTICA

SMALLEST ○ BIGGEST

① THE PEEL P50

THE SMALLEST PRODUCTION CAR

Mini-sized, with 3 wheels, 2 doors, and a single seat, it was produced between 1962 and 1965, and only 50 units were made.

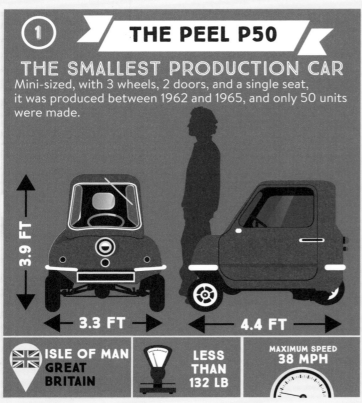

3.9 FT

3.3 FT

4.4 FT

ISLE OF MAN GREAT BRITAIN

LESS THAN 132 LB

MAXIMUM SPEED 38 MPH

② MS HARMONY OF THE SEAS

216.5 FT

WELCOME ABOARD A FLOATING ISLAND!

236.2 FT

THE LARGEST CRUISE SHIP

Launched in May 2016, this cruise ship contains 2,747 cabins, and offers its 6,780 passengers 24 elevators, 18 restaurants, 2 climbing walls, 4 pools, 10 hot tubs, 3 waterslides, 1 casino, 1 nightclub, 1 spa, 1 ice rink, 1 amusement park, 1 basketball court, and 1 mini-golf course!

WEIGHT: 223,414 TONS
550 TONS OF PAINT
66,000 TONS OF STEEL

3,300 MI OF ELECTRIC CABLE

SAINT-NAZAIRE FRANCE

1,188 FT LONG (IN COMPARISON, THE EIFFEL TOWER IS 1,062 FT TALL, INCLUDING THE ANTENNA.)

6.4 MILLION SQ FT (112 AMERICAN FOOTBALL FIELDS)

③ THE TRADINNO ROBOT

THE LARGEST WALKING ROBOT

3.9 FT OF ELECTRIC CABLES

238 SENSORS

26.9 FT

49.2 FT

ZANDT GERMANY

12 TONS

Incredibly life-like, it was created to be used in theatrical performances.

④ THE AMERICAN DREAM

THE LONGEST LIMOUSINE

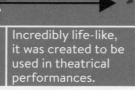

675 MPH

617 TONS

FRANCE

853 PASSENGERS

THE LARGEST PASSENGER PLANE
Operating since 2005, the A380 can go halfway around the world without refueling.

⑤ THE AIRBUS A380

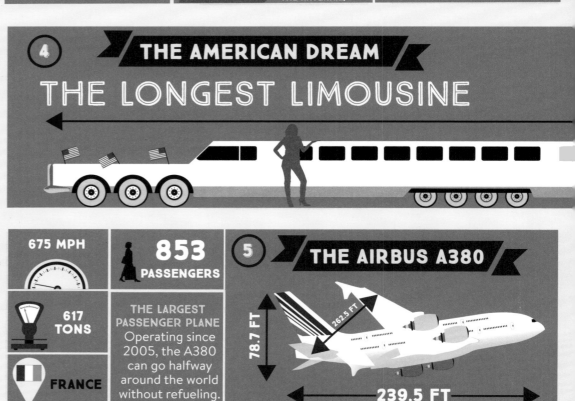

78.7 FT

262.5 FT

239.5 FT

⑥ THE GRAN ARTIC 300

THE LARGEST BUS

This bus was created by Volvo, a Swedish company. It made its debut at the 2016 FetransRio expo in Brazil, where the buses have already hit the streets.

3 ARTICULATED SECTIONS

The equivalent of 3 buses

8 WHEELS

300 PASSENGERS

SWEDEN

98.4 FT

7 MINIATUR WUNDERLAND

THE LARGEST
MODEL RAILWAY

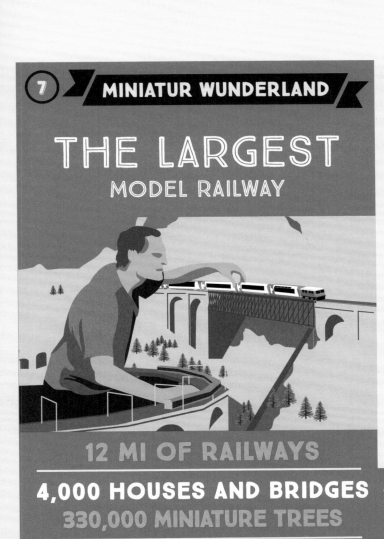

12 MI OF RAILWAYS

4,000 HOUSES AND BRIDGES
330,000 MINIATURE TREES
65,000 SQ FT | 1,300 TRAINS
600,000 MAN-HOURS SPENT
TO BUILD IT

Created in 2000 by twin brothers Gerrit and Frederik Braun, this rail system is one of the most famous attractions in Germany.

HAMBURG GERMANY

UNITS MANU-FACTURED: 1

1 pivot joint in the middle to help with steering and turns

24 WHEELS
1 JACUZZI
1 DOUBLE BED

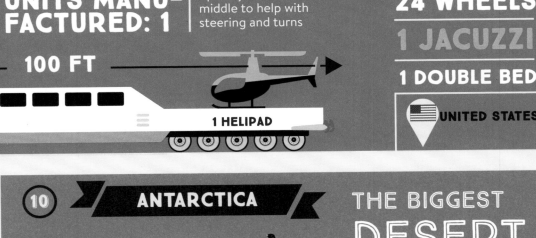

100 FT

1 HELIPAD

UNITED STATES

---

8 THE ARCTIC WILLOW

THE SMALLEST TREE

BETWEEN 0.8 AND 4.0 IN

MOST EATEN BY:

The caribou

The Arctic hare

The musk ox

It grows in the northernmost region of our planet and is one of the few plants able to withstand the dry and freezing climate of the Arctic.

HIGH ARCTIC

THE TALLEST TREE
ANNUAL GROWTH: 1.2 IN

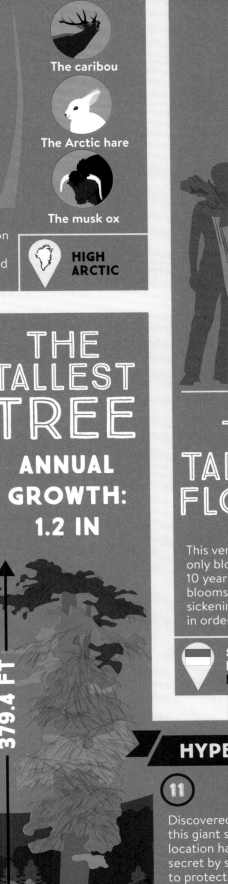

379.4 FT

TOP SECRET

THE TITAN ARUM 9

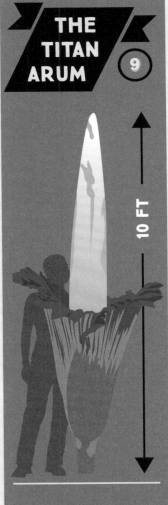

10 FT

THE TALLEST FLOWER

This very rare plant only blooms once every 10 years. When it blooms, it releases a sickening stench in order to attract flies.

SUMATRAN RAINFORESTS INDONESIA

---

11 HYPERION

Discovered in 2006, this giant sequoia's exact location has been kept secret by scientists in order to protect it.

AGE:
600 YEARS
OLD

3,637 TONS

REDWOOD NATIONAL PARK THE UNITED STATES

---

10 ANTARCTICA

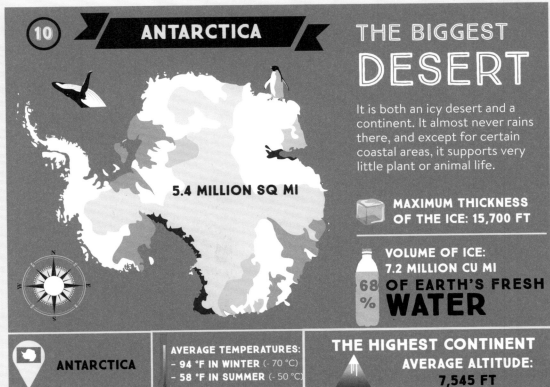

5.4 MILLION SQ MI

THE BIGGEST DESERT

It is both an icy desert and a continent. It almost never rains there, and except for certain coastal areas, it supports very little plant or animal life.

MAXIMUM THICKNESS OF THE ICE: 15,700 FT

VOLUME OF ICE: 7.2 MILLION CU MI
68% **OF EARTH'S FRESH WATER**

ANTARCTICA

AVERAGE TEMPERATURES:
- 94 °F IN WINTER (- 70 °C)
- 58 °F IN SUMMER (- 50 °C)

THE HIGHEST CONTINENT AVERAGE ALTITUDE: 7,545 FT

12 ARMILLARIA MELLEA HUMONGOUS FUNGUS

THE LARGEST LIVING ORGANISM IS A GIANT MUSHROOM!

This parasitic mushroom spreads underground and then surfaces to form clusters around the bases of the trees that it feeds off. In the Blue Mountains, 112 trees have been killed by this mushroom.

AGE: 2,400 YEARS OLD

OREGON UNITED STATES

3.72 MI² = 1,800 American football fields

13 MOUNT EVEREST

THE HIGHEST MOUNTAIN ON EARTH
29,029 FT

MAY 29, 1953: FIRST SUCCESSFUL **ASCENT**

FASTEST ASCENT COMPLETED IN **8 HOURS 10 MINUTES (2004)**

18 CLIMBING PATHS

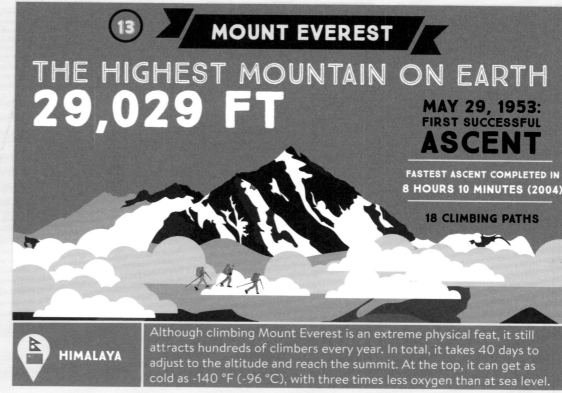

HIMALAYA

Although climbing Mount Everest is an extreme physical feat, it still attracts hundreds of climbers every year. In total, it takes 40 days to adjust to the altitude and reach the summit. At the top, it can get as cold as -140 °F (-96 °C), with three times less oxygen than at sea level.

14 TAMU MASSIF

It is nearly the size of the solar system's largest volcano, the Olympus Mons, found on Mars.

Until its discovery in 2013, no one even imagined there was a mega-volcano hidden at the bottom of the ocean. Luckily, it has been dormant for millions of years.

PACIFIC OCEAN

145 MILLION YEARS

THE BIGGEST VOLCANO

280 MI WIDE AND 400 MI LONG

15 CHANDRA BAHADUR DANGI

THE SHORTEST PERSON EVER

THE AVERAGE SIZE OF A TWO-MONTH-OLD BABY

24.1 IN

NEPAL

24.6 LB

November 30, 1939–September 4, 2015

16 JYOTI AMGE

THE SHORTEST WOMAN EVER

Jyoti was born with achondroplasia, which restricts her growth and height. She makes frequent TV appearances, and in 2011, she played a role in a popular American TV series.

24.7 IN

Born: December 16, 1993

INDIA

13.2 LB

ROBERT PERSHING WADLOW

THE TALLEST MAN IN HISTORY

Shoe size: 19

12.7 IN

18.5 IN

Due to an abnormally high production of growth hormone, he continued to grow until the day he died.

5 FT 5 IN at 5 years old

6 FT 6 IN at 10 years old

7 FT 10 IN at 16 years old

HEIGHT CHART

8 FT 11 IN at 22 years old

UNITED STATES

438.7 LB

Lived: February 22, 1918–July 15, 1940

18 HANS N. LANGSETH

THE LONGEST BEARD

Following Langseth's death in 1927, his beard was donated to the Smithsonian, a scientific institution in Washington, D.C.

NORWAY

17.49 FT

19 NICK STOEBERL

THE LONGEST TONGUE

3.98 IN

It is nearly half an inch longer than the average tongue.

CALIFORNIA UNITED STATES

20 MEHMET ÖZYÜREK

THE LONGEST NOSE

3.46 IN

ARTVIN TURKEY

This man from a small Turkish city has the longest nose ever recorded.

THE PYGMY MARMOSET

22 THE WORLD'S SMALLEST MONKEY

4.7 TO 5.9 IN

Despite its tiny size, this so-called "pocket monkey" can jump up to 12 feet high!

3.5 OZ

THE AMAZON SOUTH AMERICA

WEIGHT AT BIRTH:
ABOUT 0.5 OZ

21 SIDDIQA PARVEEN

THE TALLEST WOMAN

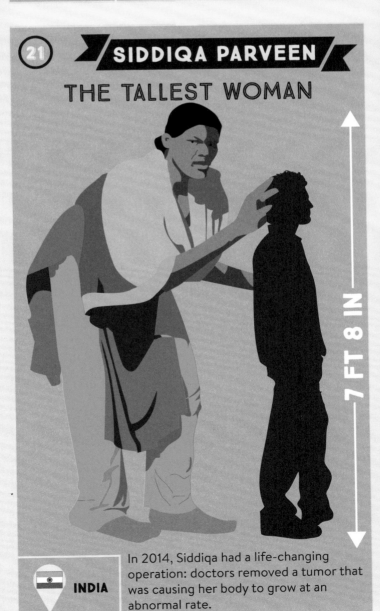

7 FT 8 IN

INDIA

In 2014, Siddiqa had a life-changing operation: doctors removed a tumor that was causing her body to grow at an abnormal rate.

23 THE NANO-FROG

0.3 IN
smaller than a thumbnail

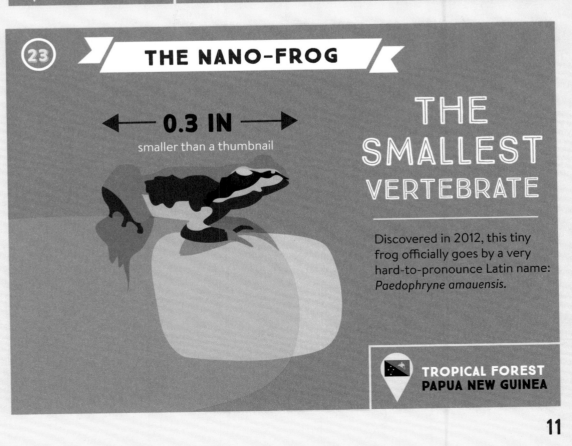

THE SMALLEST VERTEBRATE

Discovered in 2012, this tiny frog officially goes by a very hard-to-pronounce Latin name: *Paedophryne amauensis*.

TROPICAL FOREST PAPUA NEW GUINEA

THE MICRO-WASP

24

This tiny wasp belongs to the species *Dicopomorpha echmepterygis*. The record is actually held by the male, who is blind, wingless, and much smaller than the female.

THE SMALLEST INSECT

FEMALE

The females are 40% larger than the males.

MALE

0.005 IN (the width of a hair)

 DISCOVERED IN
1997

 COSTA RICA

26

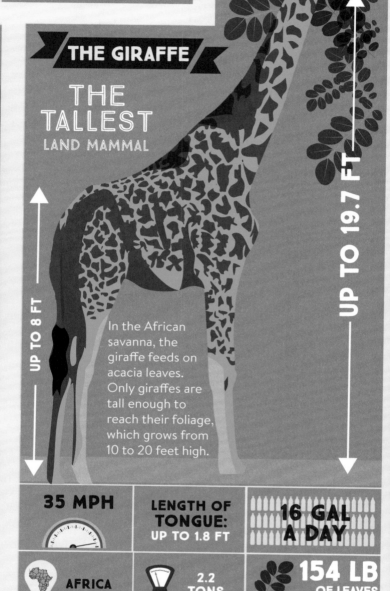

THE WHALE SHARK

25

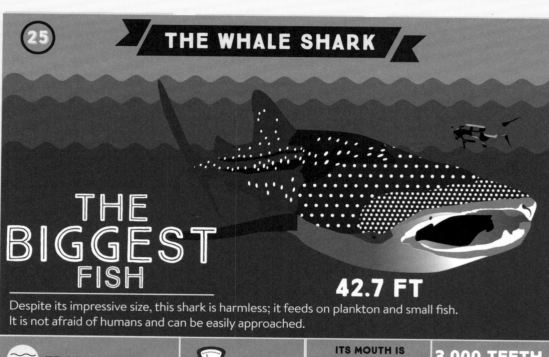

THE BIGGEST FISH

42.7 FT

Despite its impressive size, this shark is harmless; it feeds on plankton and small fish. It is not afraid of humans and can be easily approached.

TROPICAL AND TEMPERATE SEAS	11 TONS	ITS MOUTH IS **4.9 FT WIDE.**	**3,000 TEETH,** SKIN IS **3.9 IN THICK**

THE GIRAFFE

THE TALLEST LAND MAMMAL

UP TO 19.7 FT

UP TO 8 FT

In the African savanna, the giraffe feeds on acacia leaves. Only giraffes are tall enough to reach their foliage, which grows from 10 to 20 feet high.

35 MPH	LENGTH OF TONGUE: UP TO 1.8 FT	**16 GAL A DAY**
AFRICA	**2.2 TONS**	**154 LB** OF LEAVES A DAY

THE GOLIATH BIRDEATER

27

THE BIGGEST SPIDER

With a body the size of a fist and a leg span the size of an adult forearm, the Goliath birdeater mostly hunts prey larger than itself, such as small mammals and frogs. Interestingly, this massive tarantula rarely eats birds, despite its name.

12 IN
(the size of a dinner plate)

FANGS 1 IN LONG

6 OZ	**3 EGGS**

 THE AMAZON SOUTH AMERICA

THE GREAT DANE

28

THE LARGEST DOG EVER

Zeus, the largest dog on record, was a Great Dane, a breed of dogs known for their gargantuan proportions.

3.87 FT
(bigger than a Shetland pony)

15 LB OF DOG FOOD/ **WEEK**

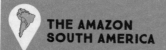 UNITED STATES	154 LB	 LIVED FROM 2007-2014

THE TEACUP YORKSHIRE TERRIER

29

THE SMALLEST DOG EVER

3.7 IN

2.8 IN

With more than 340 official breeds, dogs are the animal that vary the most in size. The smallest dog ever recorded was a teacup Yorkshire terrier named Sylvia.

UNITED KINGDOM	7 OZ	 BORN IN 1942

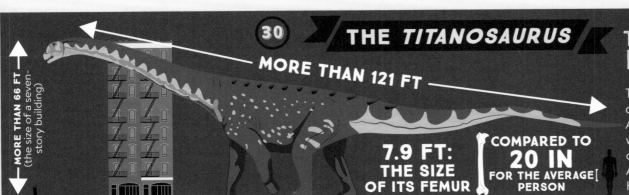

30 THE *TITANOSAURUS*

THE BIGGEST DINOSAUR

MORE THAN 121 FT

MORE THAN 66 FT (the size of a seven-story building)

7.9 FT: THE SIZE OF ITS FEMUR | COMPARED TO **20 IN** FOR THE AVERAGE PERSON

The bones of this enormous dinosaur were found in Argentina in 2014. Its skeleton was reconstructed and is currently on exhibit at the American Museum of Natural History in New York City.

 **NEARLY 77 TONS** (the equivalent of 10 elephants)

 AGE: MORE THAN **100 MILLION YEARS OLD**

 PATAGONIA ARGENTINA

---

31 THE *MICRORAPTOR ZHAOIANUS*

THE SMALLEST DINOSAUR

15 IN (the size of a pigeon)

An early ancestor of birds, it had four wings, each covered in feathers. It was also one of the smallest dinosaurs. It flew by gliding and was able to climb trees.

IN THE FILM *AVATAR*, THE WAY THE BANSHEES FLY WAS INSPIRED BY HOW THESE LITTLE DINOSAURS ARE THOUGHT TO FLY.

 CHINA | MOST LIKELY **120 MILLION YEARS OLD** | DATE OF DISCOVERY: **2000**

---

32 THE *ABELISAURUS* FOOTPRINT

THE BIGGEST DINOSAUR FOOTPRINT

3.9 FT (2 times the size of an elephant footprint)

39 FT

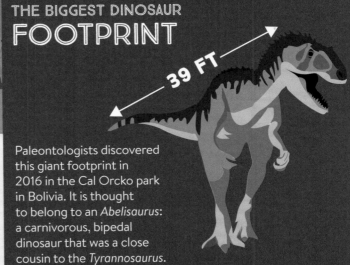

Paleontologists discovered this giant footprint in 2016 in the Cal Orcko park in Bolivia. It is thought to belong to an *Abelisaurus*: a carnivorous, bipedal dinosaur that was a close cousin to the *Tyrannosaurus*.

 BOLIVIA | DATING FROM ABOUT 70 TO 80 MILLION YEARS AGO

---

34 ONE WORLD TRADE CENTER

THE TALLEST TOWER IN THE UNITED STATES

Constructed on the site of the former World Trade Center, which was destroyed during the September 11 terrorist attack, it is also commonly referred to as the Freedom Tower.

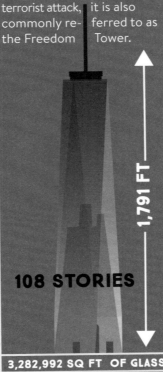

1,791 FT

108 STORIES

3,282,992 SQ FT OF GLASS
52,911 TONS OF STEEL
220,462 TONS OF CONCRETE

 CONSTRUCTION TIME: **7 YEARS** (2006–2013)

OPENED TO THE PUBLIC ON NOVEMBER 3, 2014
ARCHITECT: DAVID CHILDS

 NEW YORK UNITED STATES

---

33 KERET HOUSE

THE SMALLEST HOUSE

Constructed in 2012, this house is so narrow you could walk by without even noticing it! Owned by the author and director Etgar Keret, the smallest house in the world is also an artist residency.

3.94 FT

150 SQ FT TOTAL SURFACE AREA (the size of a bedroom)

2 STORIES, 1 BEDROOM, 1 KITCHEN, 1 BATHROOM

7 PEOPLE: THE MAXIMUM AMOUNT OF PEOPLE WHO CAN FIT IN THE HOUSE

 WARSAW POLAND | ARCHITECT: JAKUB SZCZĘSNY | CONSTRUCTION DATE: **2012**

---

35 BURJ KHALIFA

THE TALLEST FREE-STANDING STRUCTURE

The Burj Khalifa is currently the tallest free-standing structure ever built. It contains offices, a hotel, restaurants, and luxury boutiques.

163 STORIES

42,990 TONS OF STEEL BEAMS

1,528,475 SQ FT OF GLASS FOR THE FACADE

57 OF THE FASTEST ELEVATORS IN THE WORLD (22 mi per hour)

22 MILLION MAN-HOURS

2,716 FT

 DUBAI UNITED ARAB EMIRATES | ARCHITECTS: SKIDMORE, OWINGS & MERRILL | TIME TO CONSTRUCT: **6 YEARS** (2004–2010)

MILL ENDS PARK

THE SMALLEST PARK

This small piece of protected land was created for a St. Patrick's Day party, where it was meant to host a colony of imaginary creatures from Irish folklore—leprechauns!

**24 IN DIAMETER
3.14 SQ FT**

The size of a flower pot

 **CREATION DATE:
1948**

 **PORTLAND
UNITED STATES**

(36)

---

(37)

THE POOL IN ALGARROBO

ONE OF THE LARGEST POOLS

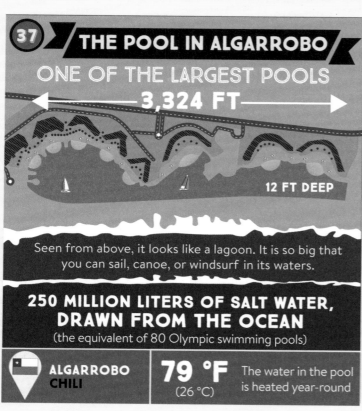

← 3,324 FT →

12 FT DEEP

Seen from above, it looks like a lagoon. It is so big that you can sail, canoe, or windsurf in its waters.

250 MILLION LITERS OF SALT WATER, DRAWN FROM THE OCEAN
(the equivalent of 80 Olympic swimming pools)

**ALGARROBO
CHILI**

79 °F
(26 °C)

The water in the pool is heated year-round

---

(38)

THE ZHANGJIAJIE GLASS BRIDGE

THE LONGEST GLASS BRIDGE

Its glass bottom gives you the impression of walking on air. Made up of 99 glass panels, it can support the weight of 800 people.

Its stretches high above the Zhangjiajie Grand Canyon.

← 1,411 FT LONG →

984 FT ABOVE GROUND

← 20 FT WIDE →

**ZHANGJIAJIE
MOUNTAINS
CHINA**

**ARCHITECT:
HAIM DOTAN**

**OPENED:
2016**

---

(39)

THE OLDEST ARTWORK **IN THE LOUVRE:** AYN GHAZAL STATUES **9,000 YEARS OLD**

THE LOUVRE MUSEUM

THE LARGEST ART MUSEUM
It was a fortress and residence to the kings of France.

35,000 WORKS OF ART ON DISPLAY
460,000 WORKS PRESERVED

20,000 PEOPLE come every day to see the *Mona Lisa*, painted by Leonardo da Vinci between 1503 and 1519.

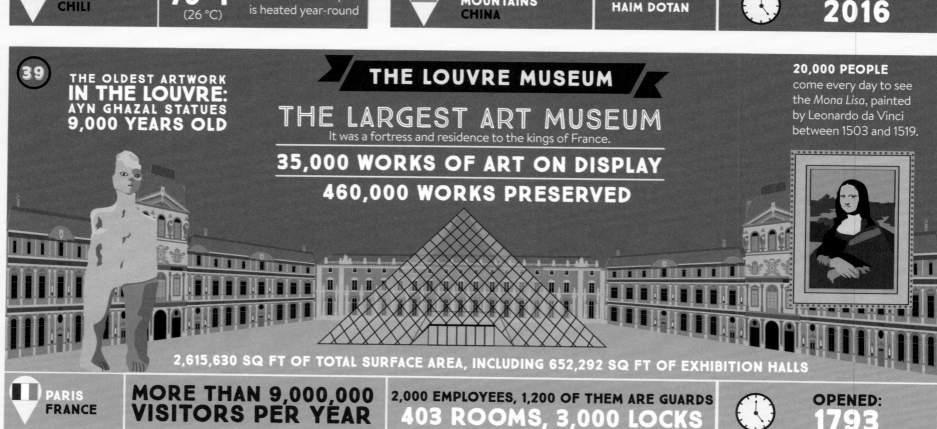

2,615,630 SQ FT OF TOTAL SURFACE AREA, INCLUDING 652,292 SQ FT OF EXHIBITION HALLS

**PARIS
FRANCE**

MORE THAN 9,000,000 VISITORS PER YEAR

2,000 EMPLOYEES, 1,200 OF THEM ARE GUARDS
403 ROOMS, 3,000 LOCKS

**OPENED:
1793**

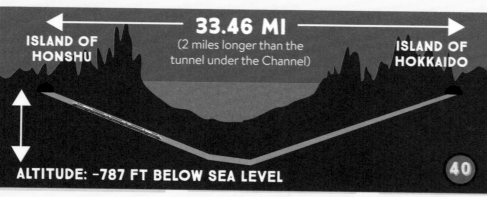

← 33.46 MI →
(2 miles longer than the tunnel under the Channel)

ISLAND OF HONSHU

ISLAND OF HOKKAIDO

ALTITUDE: -787 FT BELOW SEA LEVEL

THE SEIKAN TUNNEL

THE LONGEST AND DEEPEST UNDERSEA TUNNEL

(40)

**TSUGARU STRAIT
JAPAN**

**CONSTRUCTION TIME:
12 YEARS** (1971-1983)

41 | ISTANA NURUL IMAN

THE LARGEST INHABITED HOME

This immense palace belongs to the Sultan of Brunei. It is open to the public three days a year during Ramadan.

564 CHANDELIERS
AND 51,000 LIGHTBULBS LIGHT THE HOUSE

THE BANQUET HALL CAN ACCOMODATE 5,000 GUESTS

2,152,782 SQ FT
40 TIMES THE AREA OF THE WHITE HOUSE

1,788 ROOMS

257 BATHS
5 SWIMMING POOLS
44 STAIRWAYS
18 ELEVATORS

BANDAR SERI BEGAWAN BRUNEI

ARCHITECT: LEANDRO V. LOCSIN

42 | THE FAST TELESCOPE

THE LARGEST RADIO TELESCOPE

The five-hundred-meter Aperture Spherical Telescope also goes by the name "Heaven's Eye" in Chinese. Its mission: to study the evolution of the universe and to try and find signs of extraterrestrial life.

2,152,782 SQ FT
(the surface area of 37 American football fields)

THIS GIANT METALLIC MIRROR IS MADE UP OF 4,450 TRIANGULAR PANELS POINTED AT THE SKY, SPANNING
1,640 FT ACROSS.

GUIZHOU PROVINCE CHINA

CONSTRUCTION TIME: **5 YEARS** (2011-2016)

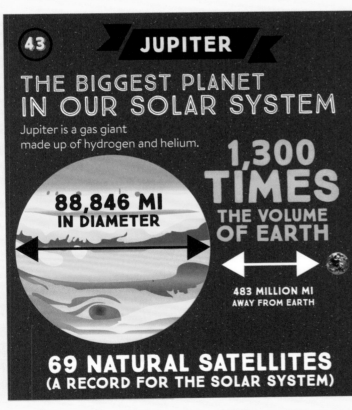

43 | JUPITER

THE BIGGEST PLANET IN OUR SOLAR SYSTEM

Jupiter is a gas giant made up of hydrogen and helium.

1,300 TIMES
THE VOLUME OF EARTH

88,846 MI IN DIAMETER

483 MILLION MI AWAY FROM EARTH

69 NATURAL SATELLITES
(A RECORD FOR THE SOLAR SYSTEM)

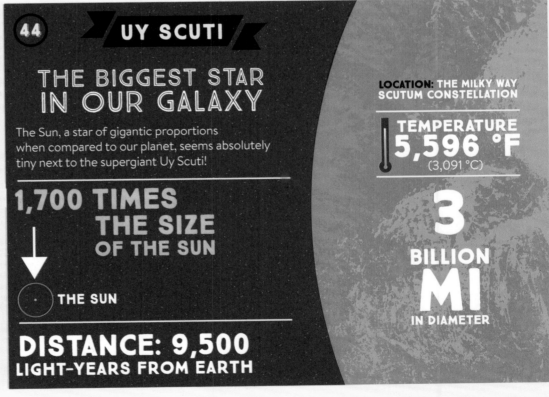

44 | UY SCUTI

THE BIGGEST STAR IN OUR GALAXY

The Sun, a star of gigantic proportions when compared to our planet, seems absolutely tiny next to the supergiant Uy Scuti!

1,700 TIMES
THE SIZE OF THE SUN

THE SUN

DISTANCE: 9,500 LIGHT-YEARS FROM EARTH

LOCATION: THE MILKY WAY SCUTUM CONSTELLATION

TEMPERATURE
5,596 °F
(3,091 °C)

3 BILLION MI
IN DIAMETER

MERCURY | MERCURY | 45

THE SMALLEST PLANET IN OUR SOLAR SYSTEM

This rocky planet is the closest to the sun.

3,032 MI IN DIAMETER (3 times smaller than the Earth)

AVERAGE TEMPERATURE: 806 °F (430 °C) DURING THE DAY

SUN | MERCURY | EARTH | JUPITER

LIGHTEST
HEAVIEST

- DINOSAURS
- ANIMALS
- HUMANS
- ARCHITECTURE
- TECHNOLOGY
- ASTRONOMY
- NATURE
- SPORTS

Weight

To know how heavy something is, you have to know its weight—or more exactly, its mass. Mass is the amount of matter in an object. Bathroom scales, kitchen scales, weighing stations—there are all kinds of scales used to weigh objects of all sizes. In the United States, weight is measured in ounces and pounds. In rest of the world, though, an object's weight (or mass) is calculated in kilograms and its variations: grams, milligrams, tonnes, etc. The United Kingdom uses a mix of the two: food is measured in grams and kilograms, and people are measured in pounds and stones!

1 KILO = 1.000 G	1 POUND = 453.592 G	1 OUNCE = 28.349 G

THE LIGHTEST	THE HEAVIEST

THE T-REX DUNG PILE
9

PANDO, THE TREMBLING GIANT
14 21

United States

ASTOLAT CASTLE

THE BEE HUMMINGBIRD
6

Cuba

Pacific Ocean

THE ARGENTINOSAURUS

THE BLUE WHALE
3

10 Argentina

THE BAGGER 293

THE BELAZ
75710 TRUCK

EDDIE HALL

England

THE PUMPKIN

Germany

Belarus

ÔRORA

Russia

20

11

15

16

18

Belgium

France

THE
COLOMBAN
CRI-CRI

THE
ANTONOV
AN-225
MRIYA

17

7

THE ETRUSCAN
SHREW

FLOWERS
OF THE FOUR
SEASONS

Japan

22

23

THE JACKFRUIT

13

THE BUMBLEBEE BAT

8

Thailand

USHIKU
DAIBUTSU

India

5

THE AFRICAN
BUSH
ELEPHANT

4

Indian

Ocean

THE HOBA
METEORITE

1

Namibia

12

South Africa

THE OSTRICH

THE CULLINAN DIAMOND

Atlantic

Ocean

THE INTERNATIONAL SPACE STATION

2

LIGHTEST
HEAVIEST

1 THE HEAVIEST METEORITE

THE HOBA METEORITE

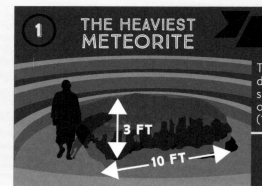

This rock from outer space, discovered in 1920, is a sight to be seen. It is made of iron (82.4%), nickel (16.4%), and cobalt.

3 FT
10 FT

66 TONS

DATE OF ITS ARRIVAL ON EARTH: 80,000 YEARS AGO

GROOTFONTEIN NAMIBIA

2 THE INTERNATIONAL SPACE STATION (ISS)

THE MOST MASSIVE OBJECT ASSEMBLED IN SPACE

It permanently houses 6 astronauts whose job is to observe Earth and the universe, and to conduct scientific experiments. The 440 tons of material that make up the different modules were delivered by over 40 space shuttle launches.

496 TONS

THE ISS ORBITS **THE EARTH AN AVERAGE OF 15 TIMES EVERY 24 HOURS.**

240 FT

Platform as big as a football field

354 FT

15 COUNTRIES	**CONSTRUCTION:** 13 YEARS (1998–2011)	**SUPPLIES VIA CARGO DELIVERY:** 2.2 TO 6.6 TONS OF FUEL, WATER, OXYGEN, AND EQUIPMENT	**ALTITUDE:** BETWEEN 217 AND 249 MI

3 THE BLUE WHALE

THE BIGGEST LIVING ANIMAL

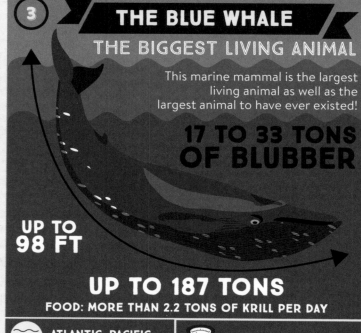

This marine mammal is the largest living animal as well as the largest animal to have ever existed!

17 TO 33 TONS OF BLUBBER

UP TO **98 FT**

UP TO 187 TONS
FOOD: MORE THAN 2.2 TONS OF KRILL PER DAY

ATLANTIC, PACIFIC, INDIAN, AND ANTARCTIC OCEANS	**WEIGHT AT BIRTH:** 3.3 TONS

4 THE OSTRICH

UP TO 9 FT

UP TO 330 LB

Weight, size, speed ... The ostrich has racked up the records!

THE HEAVIEST BIRD

AFRICA	**44 MPH** (faster than a galloping horse)	**WEIGHT OF EGG:** 4.2 LB

5 THE AFRICAN BUSH ELEPHANT

THE LARGEST LAND MAMMAL

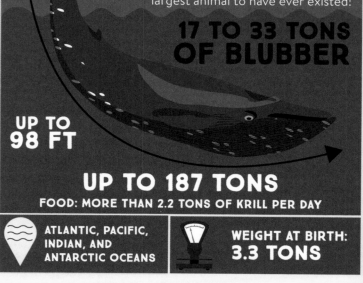

This heavyweight champion of the African savanna is twice as heavy as its cousin, the African forest elephant.

11.5 FT

UP TO 7.7 TONS

AFRICA	**WEIGHT OF A TUSK:** 198 LB	**WEIGHT AT BIRTH:** 243 LB	**IT EATS MORE THAN 440 LB** OF LEAVES AND DRINKS 26 GAL OF **WATER EVERY DAY.**

6 THE BEE HUMMINGBIRD

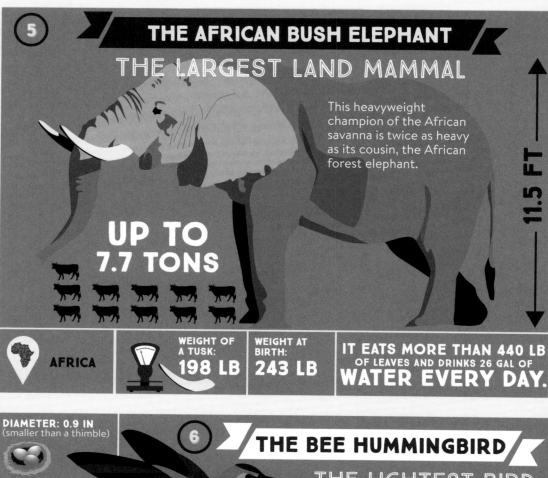

THE LIGHTEST BIRD

The size of an insect, the bee hummingbird is a strong flier and can beat its wings 80 times per second.

WEIGHT OF ADULT: BETWEEN 0.05 AND 0.07 OZ
= 2 PAPERCLIPS

2.2 IN

DIAMETER: 0.9 IN (smaller than a thimble)

WEIGHT OF EGG: 0.02 OZ (the smallest egg in the world)

CUBA

WEIGHT AT BIRTH:
0.008 OZ

IT EATS 0.18 OZ OF FOOD A DAY
(twice its body weight)

AFRICA, EUROPE, ASIA,

⑦ **THE ETRUSCAN SHREW**

THE LIGHTEST MAMMAL

This small, insect-eating mammal is hard to spot: it is tiny, and it only comes out at night!

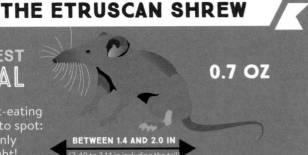

0.7 OZ

BETWEEN 1.4 AND 2.0 IN
(2.40 to 3.14 in including the tail)

⑧ **THE BUMBLEBEE BAT**

THE LIGHTEST MAMMAL

0.07 OZ

Discovered in a cave in 1973, it is now considered the world's smallest mammal. It is tied with the Etruscan shrew for the title of lightest. It also goes by the name "Kitti's hog-nosed bat."

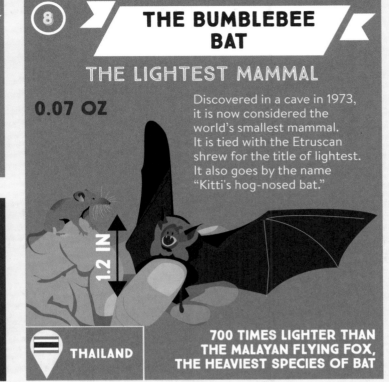

1.2 IN

THAILAND

700 TIMES LIGHTER THAN THE MALAYAN FLYING FOX, THE HEAVIEST SPECIES OF BAT

⑨ **THE *T-REX* DUNG PILE**

THE BIGGEST COPROLITE

15 LB

This fossilized dinosaur dropping is on exhibit at the Royal Saskatchewan Museum.

Judging from the little bones found inside, this giant doo-doo is thought to belong to a *Tyrannosaurus*.

7.7 TONS

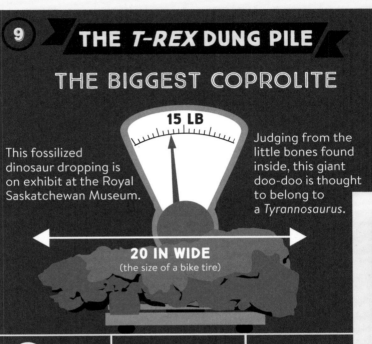

20 IN WIDE
(the size of a bike tire)

REGINA CANADA

AGE: 65 MILLION YEARS OLD

DISCOVERED IN 1995

⑩ **THE *ARGENTINOSAURUS***

131 FT

THE HEAVIEST DINOSAUR

26 FT

BETWEEN 77 AND 88 TONS

Discovered in Argentina in 1990, the bones of the Argentinosaurus revealed that the giant herbivore was not the biggest of all the dinosaurs, but was indeed the heaviest dinosaur that ever lived.

ARGENTINA

LIVED: 94 MILLION YEARS AGO

5 MPH
(10 times slower than a gazelle)

⑪ **THE PUMPKIN**

THE BIGGEST PUMPKIN

Squashes, like pumpkins, are the largest farmed vegetable. Every year a competition is held, and in 2016, the heaviest pumpkin ever was weighed.

2,624.6 LB
= the weight of 328 large pumpkins

18.77 FT IN CIRCUMFERENCE

BELGIUM

Enough to make more than 6,900 servings of pumpkin pie!

NAME OF WINNER: MATHIAS WILLEMIJNS

⑫ **THE CULLINAN DIAMOND**

THE LARGEST
ROUGH DIAMOND EVER FOUND

21.91 OUNCES
= 3,105 CARATS

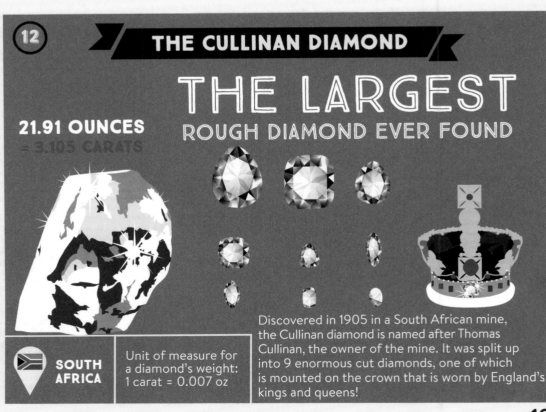

SOUTH AFRICA

Unit of measure for a diamond's weight: 1 carat = 0.007 oz

Discovered in 1905 in a South African mine, the Cullinan diamond is named after Thomas Cullinan, the owner of the mine. It was split up into 9 enormous cut diamonds, one of which is mounted on the crown that is worn by England's kings and queens!

13 · THE JACKFRUIT

THE HEAVIEST FRUIT

HEIGHT OF TREE: UP TO 66 FT TALL

UP TO **66 LB**

(the weight of 16 pineapples)

UP TO 28 IN LONG

INDIA

This fruit, native to India, develops directly on the trunk of the jackfruit tree!

14 · PANDO, THE TREMBLING GIANT

THE HEAVIEST LIVING ORGANISM

Its name means "I spread out" in Latin. Pando is a clonal colony: every tree is a clone of the same tree, and they are all interconnected by an underground network of roots.

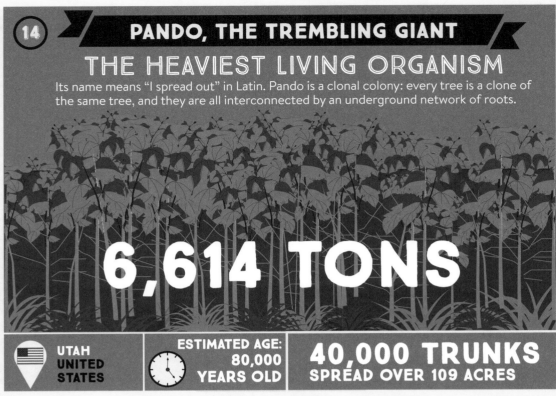

6,614 TONS

UTAH UNITED STATES

ESTIMATED AGE: **80,000 YEARS OLD**

40,000 TRUNKS SPREAD OVER 109 ACRES

15 · THE BAGGER 293

THE HEAVIEST LAND VEHICLE

Constructed in 1995, this truck is used for open-pit mining. Its mission: to dig and clear more than 8,475,520 cu ft of earth every day!

15,653 TONS = 25 AIRBUS A380S

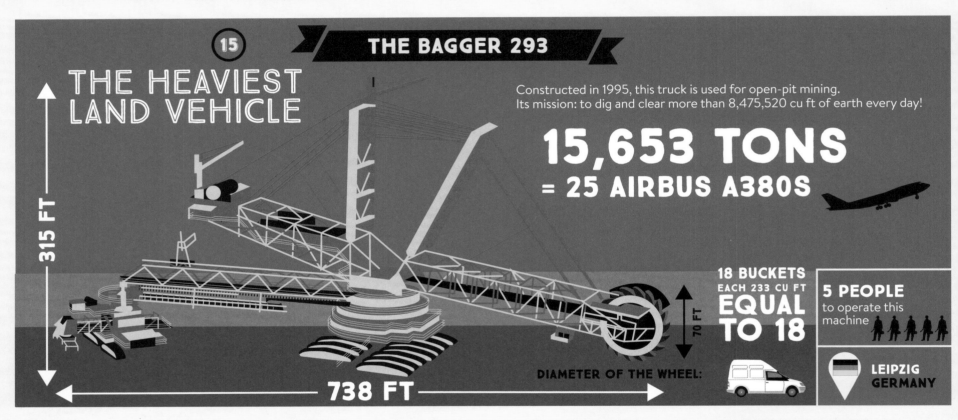

315 FT

738 FT

70 FT

DIAMETER OF THE WHEEL:

18 BUCKETS EACH 233 CU FT **EQUAL TO 18**

5 PEOPLE to operate this machine

LEIPZIG GERMANY

16 · THE BELAZ 75710 TRUCK

THE LARGEST TRUCK

It was constructed in 2013 to load, haul, and dump waste rock at a coal mine in Siberia.

893 TONS

67.6 FT

BELARUS

MAX SPEED: **40 MPH**

Haul capacity: **496 TONS**

17 · THE ANTONOV AN-225 MRIYA

THE HEAVIEST, WIDEST, AND LONGEST PLANE

The Antonov An-225 is nicknamed Mriya, which means "dream" in Ukrainian. It has been in service since 1988 and is big and strong enough to carry a spacecraft on its back!

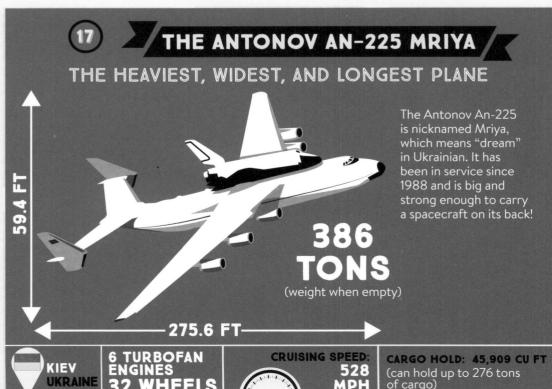

59.4 FT

386 TONS

(weight when empty)

275.6 FT

KIEV UKRAINE

6 TURBOFAN ENGINES 32 WHEELS

CRUISING SPEED: **528 MPH**

CARGO HOLD: 45,909 CU FT (can hold up to 276 tons of cargo)

18. THE COLOMBAN CRI-CRI

THE LIGHTEST TWIN-ENGINE SINGLE-SEATER AIRCRAFT

13.45 FT

176 LB
(average weight of a grown man)

Invented in 1973 by the aeronautical engineer Michel Colomban, the Cri-Cri is a "homebuilt aircraft"—you assemble it yourself!

| FRANCE | CRUISING SPEED: 106 MPH | 2,000 HOURS TO CONSTRUCT |

19. ŌRORA

6 FT 4 IN

598 LB
(nearly twice the average weight of a sumo wrestler)

THE HEAVIEST SPORTSMAN

Sumo is a Japanese style of wrestling, and its best wrestlers are often seen as demigods. Ōrora is the heaviest competing sumo wrestler, and sportsman, in the world.

8,000 TO 10,000 CALORIES A DAY
His daily intake = the equivalent of
20 BIG HAMBURGERS

RUSSIA

ASTOLAT CASTLE

21. THE LIGHTEST CASTLE

Conceived by the artist Elaine Diehl, this miniature castle is made of wood and papier-mâché. From the kitchen to the ballroom, the entire castle (which is entirely furnished and decorated) was built with extreme attention to detail.

800 LB

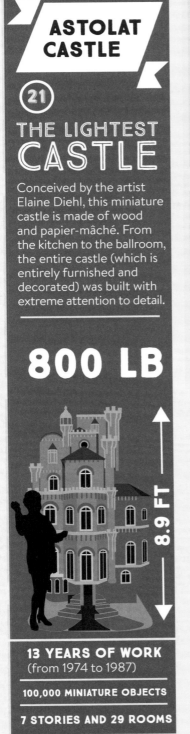

8.9 FT

13 YEARS OF WORK
(from 1974 to 1987)

100,000 MINIATURE OBJECTS

7 STORIES AND 29 ROOMS

COLORADO UNITED STATES

20. EDDIE HALL

THE STRONGEST MAN

This English strongman grabbed the world title after winning the 2017 World's Strongest Man competition. He stole the title from the four-time world champion Brian Shaw.

1,181.7 LB
Partial deadlift (18 inches off floor, with straps)

| ENGLAND | BORN JANUARY 15, 1988 | WEIGHT: 410 LB | HEIGHT: 6 FT 3 IN |

22. FLOWERS OF THE FOUR SEASONS

THE LIGHTEST BOOK EVER PRINTED

Printed by Toppan Printing using an ultra-fine printing technique, this tiny book contains pictures of flowers, with captions in Japanese. You need a magnifying glass to read it and tweezers to turn the pages!

0.03 IN

0.000017 OZ

| TOKYO JAPAN | 22 PAGES | PUBLICATION DATE: MARCH 2013 | 250 COPIES PRINTED PRICE: 235 EUROS |

USHIKU DAIBUTSU

23. THE HEAVIEST STATUE OF A DEITY

It is made entirely of bronze.

4,409 TONS

394 FT

66 FT

COMPLETED IN 1993

USHIKU JAPAN

SLOWEST
FASTEST

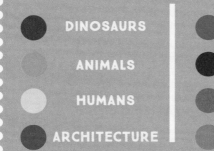

Speed

Speed refers to the distance covered in a given amount of time. Stopwatches, wind gauges, speedometers—each is a different device for measuring the speed of a runner's sprint, a gust of wind, or a speeding car. Speed is calculated in mph (miles per hour) or ft/s (feet per second). Most countries outside of the United States and United Kingdom calculate speed in km/h (kilometers per hour), while sailors measure it in knots and airplane pilots use the Mach number, Mach 1 being the speed of sound.

1 MPH (MILE PER HOUR) = 1.61 KM/H	1 KNOT = 1.15 MPH	MACH 1 = 760.5 MPH

THE SLOWEST | **THE FASTEST**

THE THRUST SCC

SATURN V

FELIX BAUMGARTNER — 13

Austria

Nevada Desert

United States

18 — 19

8

25 — USAIN BOLT

12

Jamaica

THE SR-71 BLACKBIRD

THE WATER MOCCASIN

Peru — 16

THE PUYA RAIMONDII

Pacific Ocean

4 — THE INDO-PACIFIC SAILFISH

THE THREE-TOED SLOTH

7

15

Brazil

THE PARICÁ TREE

THE HELIOS 2
PROBE
24
Germany

THE *COMPSOGNATHUS*

THE
BURGUNDY SNAIL

Europe

THE
DEINOCHEIRUS
MIRIFICUS

France

Germany

THE PEREGRINE
FALCON
2

3

17

9

21

Switzerland

Mongolia
10

THE
UTRICULARIA

THE BUGATTI
VEYRON SUPER
SPORT

THE GLACIER
EXPRESS

THE MAGLEV
TRAIN

23

Japan

1

Sahara Desert

*United
Arab Emirates*
22

14

5

THE SEAHORSE

THE SAHARAN
SILVER ANT

THE FORMULA
ROSSA

11

American Samoa

6

*Indian
Ocean*

Australia

THE CHEETAH

20

SOGELAU
TUVALU

THE *SPIRIT OF
AUSTRALIA*

*Atlantic
Ocean*

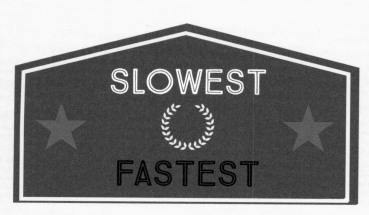

SLOWEST ⬤ FASTEST

① THE SAHARAN SILVER ANT

THE FASTEST INSECT

(in relation to its size)

This ant has longer-than-normal legs that help raise it above the burning hot sands of the Sahara.

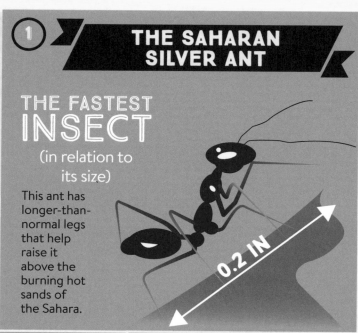

0.2 IN

 SAHARA DESERT AFRICA

1.1 MPH
(the equivalent of 100 times its size in 1 second)

② THE PEREGRINE FALCON

THE FASTEST ANIMAL IN THE WORLD

242 MPH

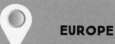 UP TO 20 IN LONG

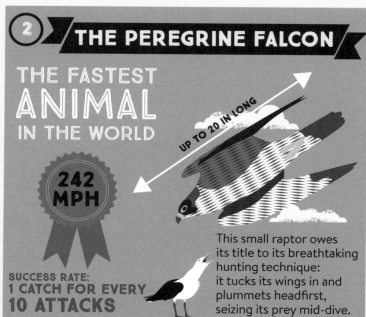

This small raptor owes its title to its breathtaking hunting technique: it tucks its wings in and plummets headfirst, seizing its prey mid-dive.

SUCCESS RATE: **1 CATCH FOR EVERY 10 ATTACKS**

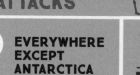 **EVERYWHERE EXCEPT ANTARCTICA**

 **19 TO 35 OZ**

2 IN

0.002 MPH

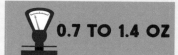 **EUROPE**

0.7 TO 1.4 OZ

③ THE BURGUNDY SNAIL

ONE OF THE SLOWEST ANIMALS

A snail is a soft-bodied mollusk protected by a shell. Instead of legs, it has a ventral foot. This foot is a muscle that contracts and extends, allowing it to slide forward on the mucous (slime) that it secretes.

3,281 FT: THE MAXIMUM DISTANCE IT CAN TRAVEL FROM HOME

④ THE INDO-PACIFIC SAILFISH

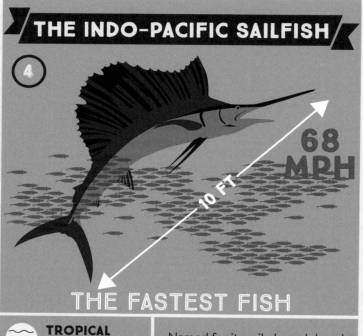

68 MPH

10 FT

THE FASTEST FISH

 TROPICAL AND TEMPERATE SEAS

Named for its sail-shaped dorsal fin, this fish reaches its record-breaking speeds while hunting.

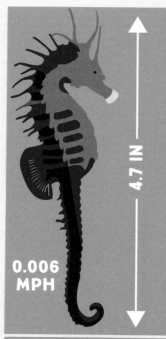

4.7 IN

0.006 MPH

 TROPICAL AND TEMPERATE SEAS

⑤ THE SEAHORSE

THE SLOWEST MARINE ANIMAL

This fish swims slowly through the water in an upright position. It steers with the pectoral fins on the sides of its head, and propels itself with a small dorsal fin, which flutters left to right 70 times a second.

⑥ THE CHEETAH

THE FASTEST LAND MAMMAL

The cheetah is made for sprinting: its lightweight body and aerodynamic build (small head, slim legs, and flattened ribcage) decrease air resistance, allowing it to reach blistering speeds.

ONE STRIDE = 23 FT

20 MIN: recovery time after a sprint

 110 LB

 AFRICA, ASIA, AND IRAN

68 MPH OVER 1,312 FT

ACCELERATION: FROM 0 TO 62 MPH IN 3 SECONDS AND 3 STRIDES (faster than a Ferrari)

UP TO 5 FT

7. THE THREE-TOED SLOTH

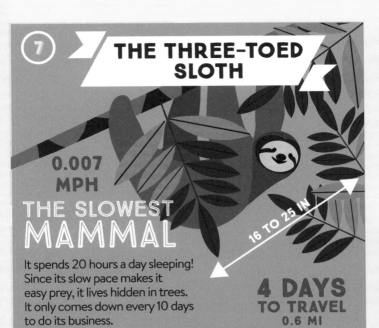

0.007 MPH

THE SLOWEST MAMMAL

It spends 20 hours a day sleeping! Since its slow pace makes it easy prey, it lives hidden in trees. It only comes down every 10 days to do its business.

16 TO 25 IN

4 DAYS TO TRAVEL 0.6 MI

SOUTH AMERICA

8.8 LB

UNIQUE FEATURE: its ability to turn its head 270° in order to look backwards without moving its body

8. THE WATER MOCCASIN

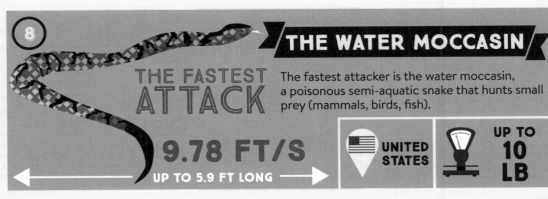

THE FASTEST ATTACK

The fastest attacker is the water moccasin, a poisonous semi-aquatic snake that hunts small prey (mammals, birds, fish).

9.78 FT/S

UP TO 5.9 FT LONG

UNITED STATES

UP TO **10 LB**

9. THE *COMPSOGNATHUS*

THE FASTEST OF ALL THE DINOSAURS

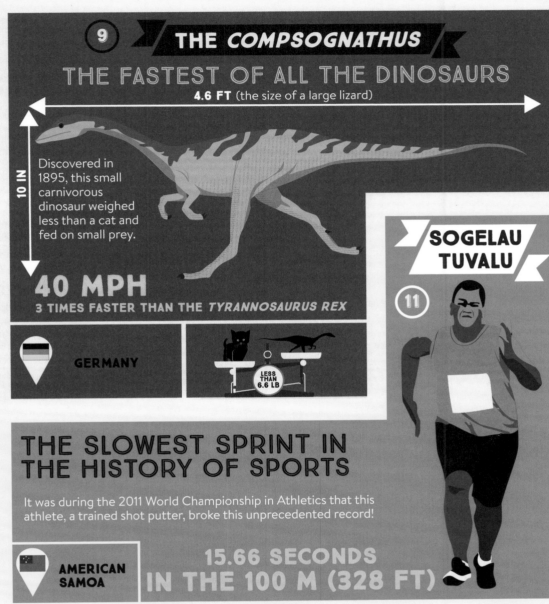

4.6 FT (the size of a large lizard)

10 IN

Discovered in 1895, this small carnivorous dinosaur weighed less than a cat and fed on small prey.

40 MPH

3 TIMES FASTER THAN THE *TYRANNOSAURUS REX*

GERMANY

LESS THAN 6.6 LB

10. THE *DEINOCHEIRUS MIRIFICUS*

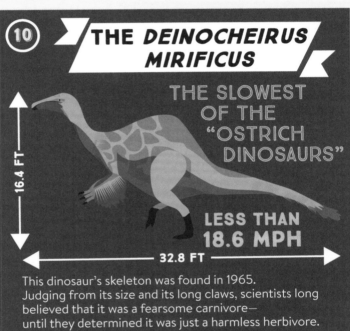

THE SLOWEST OF THE "OSTRICH DINOSAURS"

16.4 FT

32.8 FT

LESS THAN 18.6 MPH

This dinosaur's skeleton was found in 1965. Judging from its size and its long claws, scientists long believed that it was a fearsome carnivore—until they determined it was just a harmless herbivore.

THE GOBI DESERT MONGOLIA

7.7 TONS

11. SOGELAU TUVALU

THE SLOWEST SPRINT IN THE HISTORY OF SPORTS

It was during the 2011 World Championship in Athletics that this athlete, a trained shot putter, broke this unprecedented record!

AMERICAN SAMOA

15.66 SECONDS IN THE 100 M (328 FT)

12. USAIN BOLT

41 STRIDES EVERY 328 FT
(compared to an average of 44 for other sprinters)

RECORDS:
9.58 seconds
IN THE 100 M (328 FT)
19.19 seconds
IN THE 200 M (656 FT)
11-time
WORLD CHAMPION
8 Olympic gold medals

198 LB

JAMAICA

THE FASTEST MAN

This athletic champion, born August 21, 1986, is currently the world's fastest runner.

27 MPH
(maximum speed recorded mid-race)

13. FELIX BAUMGARTNER

THE FASTEST SKYDIVE

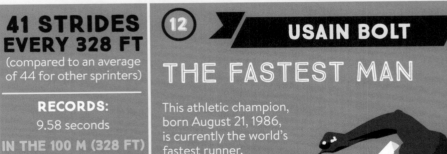

This extreme skydiver is famous for his free-fall dive on October 14, 2012, when he jumped from a helium-filled space balloon at an altitude of more than 127,952 feet. He fell so fast that he broke the sound barrier!

6 FT 5 IN

833.8 MPH
(1.24 times the speed of sound)

AUSTRIA

4 MIN 20 SEC OF FREE FALL BEFORE HIS PARACHUTE OPENED

14 THE *UTRICULARIA*

THE FASTEST CARNIVOROUS PLANT

This plant grows in swamps. Thanks to a suction effect, it captures tiny shellfish and insect larvae in record time.

1/1,000 OF A SECOND
(1 millisecond)

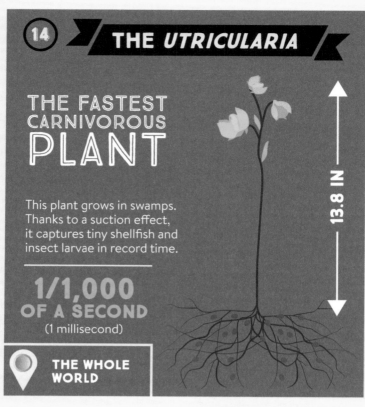

13.8 IN

📍 **THE WHOLE WORLD**

17 THE BUGATTI VEYRON SUPER SPORT

WORLD RECORD FOR FASTEST ROAD CAR

This car was created in 2010. Only 50 cars were made, all of which sold. Although other cars have gone faster, this one still holds the official record.

268 MPH
16-CYLINDER ENGINE
STRENGTH: 1,200 HORSEPOWER

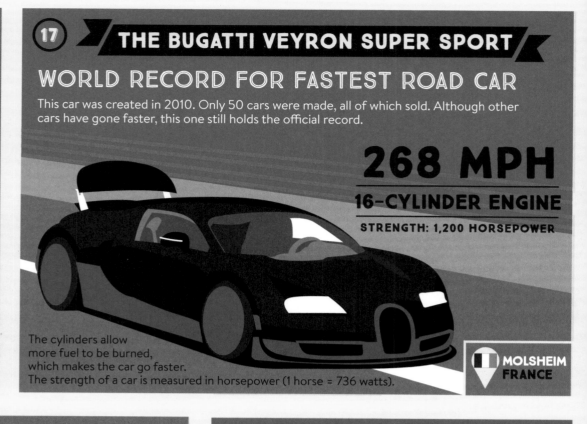

The cylinders allow more fuel to be burned, which makes the car go faster.
The strength of a car is measured in horsepower (1 horse = 736 watts).

📍 **MOLSHEIM FRANCE**

THE PARICA TREE

15 THE FASTEST GROWING TREE

131 FT

GROWTH RATE:
30 FT PER YEAR

The parica tree is grown for its wood, which is used to make plywood.
It has a formidable enemy: a cicada that prevents it from growing older than 7 years.

AVERAGE LIFE SPAN:
7 YEARS

📍 **BRAZIL**

16 THE PUYA RAIMONDII

THE SLOWEST BLOOM

This rare plant grows only in the Peruvian Andes, between 10,500 and 15,750 feet high. It blossoms only once in its life.

12 M

BLOSSOM: BETWEEN 80 AND 100 YEARS

6 MILLION SEEDS DISPERSED

📍 **PERU**

18 THE SR-71 BLACKBIRD

2,193 MPH

THE FASTEST PLANE

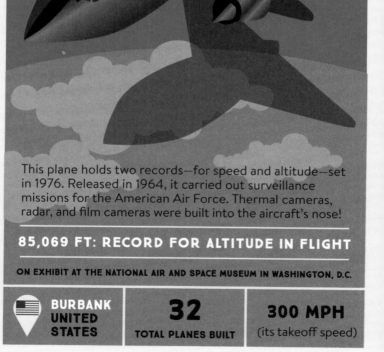

This plane holds two records—for speed and altitude—set in 1976. Released in 1964, it carried out surveillance missions for the American Air Force. Thermal cameras, radar, and film cameras were built into the aircraft's nose!

85,069 FT: RECORD FOR ALTITUDE IN FLIGHT

ON EXHIBIT AT THE NATIONAL AIR AND SPACE MUSEUM IN WASHINGTON, D.C.

📍 BURBANK UNITED STATES	**32** TOTAL PLANES BUILT	**300 MPH** (its takeoff speed)

19 THE THRUST SSC

THE FASTEST LAND VEHICLE

763.035 MPH

2 ROLLS-ROYCE TURBOJETS
POWER = 106,000 HORSEPOWER

It is basically an aerodynamic rocket on wheels. In October 1997, Andy Green, a former fighter pilot in the British Air Force, set the record in Black Rock Desert.

📍 **NEVADA UNITED STATES**

20 — THE *SPIRIT OF AUSTRALIA*

THE FASTEST BOAT

BLOWERING DAM
AUSTRALIA

6,000 HORSEPOWER

317.5 MPH
(the equivalent of 276 nautical knots)

Built by an Australian man named Ken Warby, the *Spirit of Australia* has held the water speed record since October 8, 1978.

21 — THE GLACIER EXPRESS

THE SLOWEST EXPRESS TRAIN

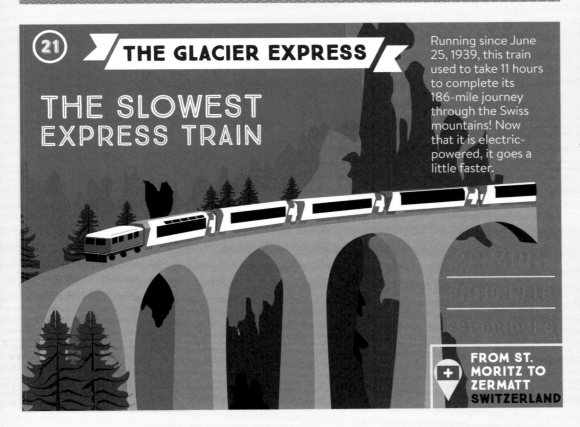

Running since June 25, 1939, this train used to take 11 hours to complete its 186-mile journey through the Swiss mountains! Now that it is electric-powered, it goes a little faster.

FROM ST. MORITZ TO ZERMATT SWITZERLAND

22 — THE FORMULA ROSSA

THE FASTEST ROLLER COASTER

149,129 MPH
in less than 5 seconds

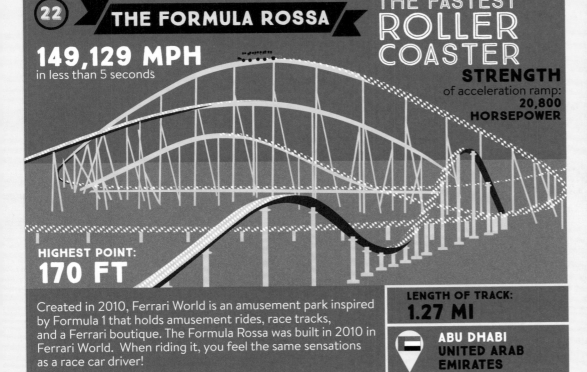

STRENGTH
of acceleration ramp:
20,800 HORSEPOWER

HIGHEST POINT:
170 FT

Created in 2010, Ferrari World is an amusement park inspired by Formula 1 that holds amusement rides, race tracks, and a Ferrari boutique. The Formula Rossa was built in 2010 in Ferrari World. When riding it, you feel the same sensations as a race car driver!

LENGTH OF TRACK:
1.27 MI

ABU DHABI
UNITED ARAB EMIRATES

23 — THE MAGLEV TRAIN

THE FASTEST TRAIN

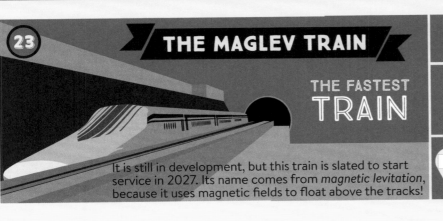

375 MPH

311 MPH
at mid speed

FROM TOKYO TO NAGOYA JAPAN

It is still in development, but this train is slated to start service in 2027. Its name comes from *magnetic levitation*, because it uses magnetic fields to float above the tracks!

24 — THE HELIOS 2 PROBE

157,078 MPH

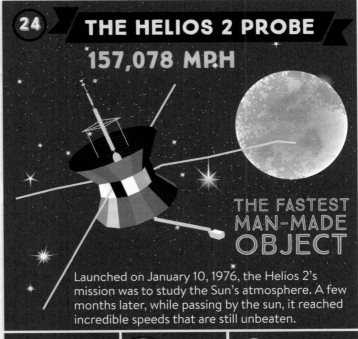

THE FASTEST MAN-MADE OBJECT

Launched on January 10, 1976, the Helios 2's mission was to study the Sun's atmosphere. A few months later, while passing by the sun, it reached incredible speeds that are still unbeaten.

RECORD SET ON APRIL 17, 1976

 830 LB

 GERMANY

25 — SATURN V

THE FASTEST A HUMAN HAS EVER TRAVELED

On May 26, 1969, during the Apollo 10 mission, 3 astronauts manning the Saturn V rocket broke the all-time record for speed just before re-entering the Earth's atmosphere.

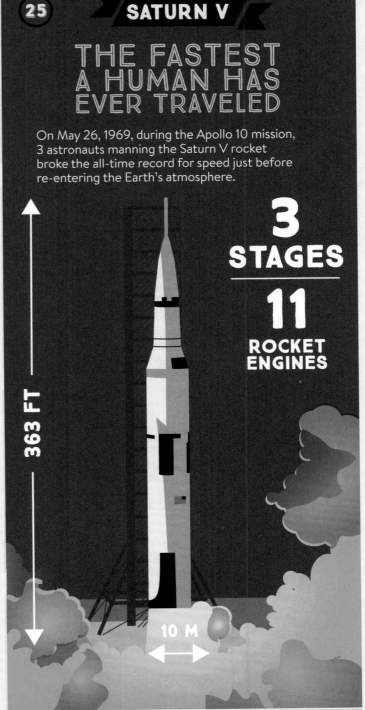

3 STAGES

11 ROCKET ENGINES

363 FT

10 M

 UNITED STATES

24,816 MPH

SHORTEST
LONGEST

DINOSAURS	TECHNOLOGY
ANIMALS	ASTRONOMY
HUMANS	NATURE
ARCHITECTURE	SPORTS

Time

The earliest instruments for measuring time were the gnomon and the sundial, which used the position of the sun—and the shadow it cast—to tell time. Later, the clepsydra and the hourglass used the flow of water or sand to measure time. For a long time they were the only instruments capable of counting minutes. Then came clocks, watches, and chronometers. These measure time much more precisely, calculating seconds, tenths of a second, or even hundredths of a second.

2000 BC: THE SUNDIAL	1300 BC: THE HOURGLASS	1930: THE QUARTZ CLOCK

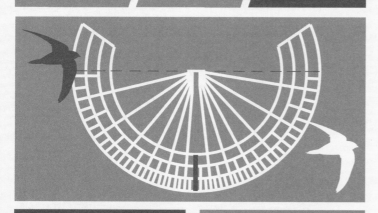

THE SHORTEST	THE LONGEST

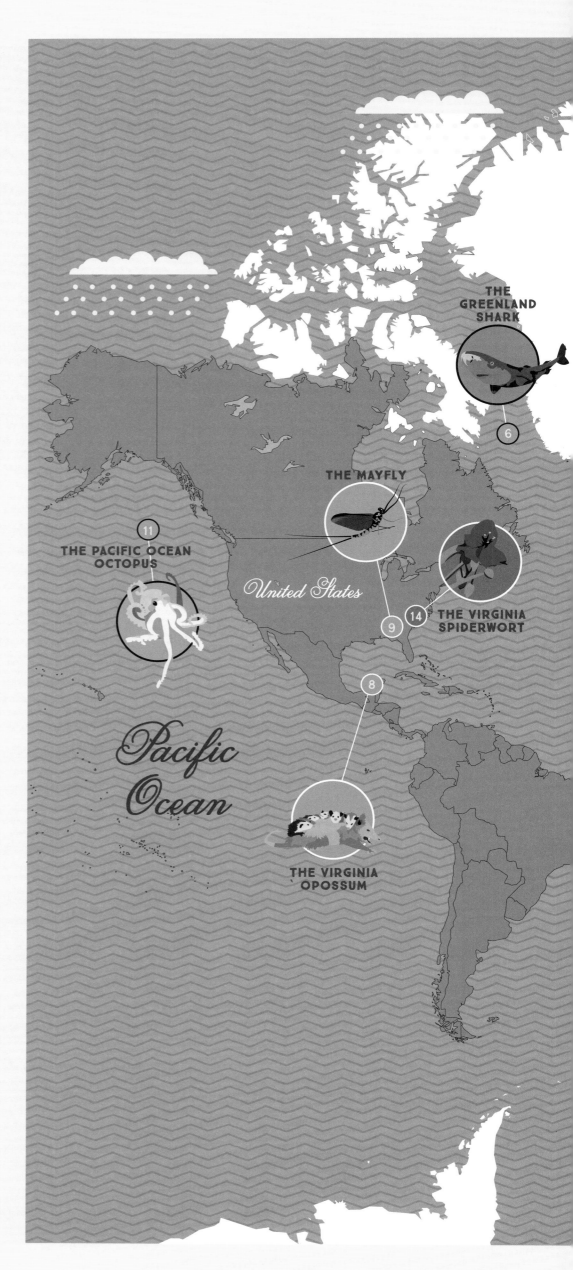

THE GREENLAND SHARK

6

THE MAYFLY

THE PACIFIC OCEAN OCTOPUS

11

United States

9

14 THE VIRGINIA SPIDERWORT

8

Pacific Ocean

THE VIRGINIA OPOSSUM

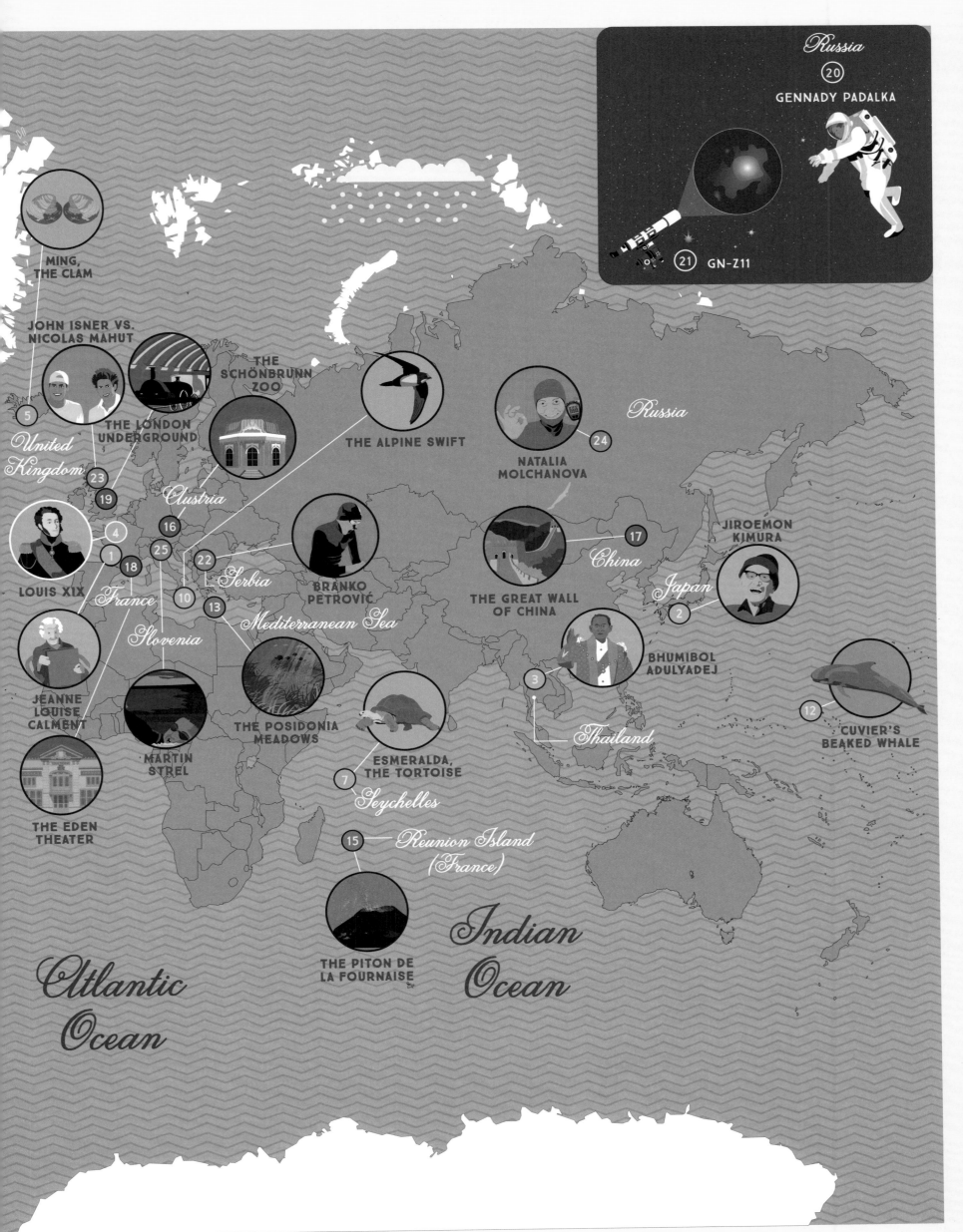

MING,
THE CLAM

JOHN ISNER VS.
NICOLAS MAHUT

5

United
Kingdom

THE SCHÖNBRUNN
ZOO

THE LONDON
UNDERGROUND

23

19

Austria

16

25

4

1

18

22

10

13

Serbia

THE ALPINE SWIFT

BRANKO
PETROVIĆ

Mediterranean Sea

LOUIS XIX

France

Slovenia

JEANNE
LOUISE
CALMENT

MARTIN
STREL

THE POSIDONIA
MEADOWS

THE EDEN
THEATER

7

Seychelles

15

ESMERALDA,
THE TORTOISE

Reunion Island
(France)

THE PITON DE
LA FOURNAISE

Atlantic
Ocean

Russia

20

GENNADY PADALKA

21 GN-Z11

NATALIA
MOLCHANOVA

24

Russia

17

China

THE GREAT WALL
OF CHINA

3

Thailand

BHUMIBOL
ADULYADEJ

JIROEMON
KIMURA

Japan

2

12

CUVIER'S
BEAKED WHALE

Indian
Ocean

SHORTEST

LONGEST

① JEANNE LOUISE CALMENT

OLDEST WOMAN TO HAVE EVER LIVED

Women dominate when it comes to longevity records! Out of everyone with a certifiable birth certificate, Jeanne Louise Calment holds the record for the longest living person ever.

MORE THAN 450,000:
THE NUMBER OF CENTENARIANS (PEOPLE 100+ YEARS OLD) WORLDWIDE IN 2018
(twice the amount in 1995)

122 YEARS
AND 164 DAYS OLD

ARLES FRANCE

FEBRUARY 21, 1875– AUGUST 4, 1997

② JIROEMON KIMURA

OLDEST MAN TO HAVE EVER LIVED

This super-centenarian is officially the longest-living man on record. He fathered 7 children and lived long enough to meet his 15 grandchildren, 25 great-grandchildren, and 13 great-great-grandchildren.

116 YEARS OLD

KYOTO JAPAN

APRIL 19, 1897– JUNE 12, 2013

③
1782: the founding of the Chakri dynasty, which still rules in Thailand.
JUNE 9, 1946: Rama IX succeeds his brother Rama VIII to the throne at the age of 19.
OCTOBER 13, 2016: upon his death, his oldest son succeeded him, under the name Rama X.

BHUMIBOL ADULYADEJ

THE LONGEST REIGN IN MODERN HISTORY

This record goes to the former king of Thailand, Bhumibol Adulyadej, better known by his royal title, Rama IX.

70 YEARS, 4 MONTHS, AND 4 DAYS

When his father, King Charles X, left the throne on August 2, 1830, Louis XIX became King of France and of Navarre just long enough give up his title as king—the very same day!

④ LOUIS XIX

THE SHORTEST REIGN
20 MIN
(the time it took to sign the document for giving up the throne)

LIVED: AUGUST 6, 1755– JUNE 3, 1844

FRANCE

REIGN: JUNE 9, 1964– OCTOBER 13, 2016

THAILAND

0.004 IN: the size of the ring that forms every year on its shell

7 YEARS: the time it took scientists to determine its age with certainty

ICELAND

2006:
THE YEAR OF ITS ACCIDENTAL DEATH, CAUSED BY THE SCIENTISTS WHO DISCOVERED IT
507 YEARS

⑤ MING, THE CLAM

3.2 IN ACROSS

THE OLDEST ANIMAL IN THE WORLD

This clam (nicknamed Ming) is a member of the species *Arctica islandica*. The scientists who studied it were able to determine its age thanks to the growth rings that formed on its shell.

BETWEEN 6.6 AND 16.4 FT

UP TO 400 YEARS OLD

⑥ THE GREENLAND SHARK

LONGEST KNOWN LIFE SPAN AMONG VERTEBRATES

Although this shark only grows 0.4 inches a year, it often grows to be 16.4 feet long. By linking its size to its age, researchers were able to estimate its life span.

IT BECOMES AN ADULT AT THE AGE OF 150	PROCESS FOR CALCULATING ITS AGE: studying the lens of the eye, as it consists of layers that build up over time	ANTARCTIC OCEAN

ESMERALDA, THE TORTOISE

7 ### THE OLDEST TORTOISE

A local star, the world's oldest tortoise freely roams an island in the Indian Ocean. She belongs to a species of giant tortoises found in the Seychelles that are known for their long life expectancy.

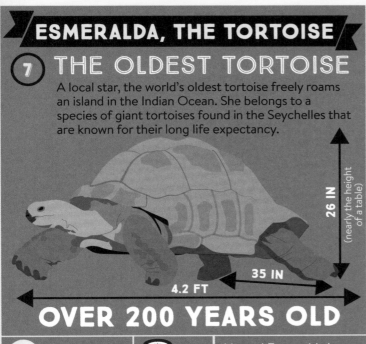

26 IN (nearly the height of a table)

4.2 FT

35 IN

OVER 200 YEARS OLD

BIRD ISLAND SEYCHELLES

794 LB

Named Esmeralda by the owners of the island, this tortoise is a male!

---

8 ## THE VIRGINIA OPOSSUM

THE SHORTEST GESTATION PERIOD

This cat-sized marsupial gives birth to its tiny babies after a gestation period of just 13 days—much shorter than most mammals. After that, the newborns continue to develop in their mother's pouch.

MINIMUM TIME SPENT IN THE MOTHER'S POUCH: 2.5 MONTHS

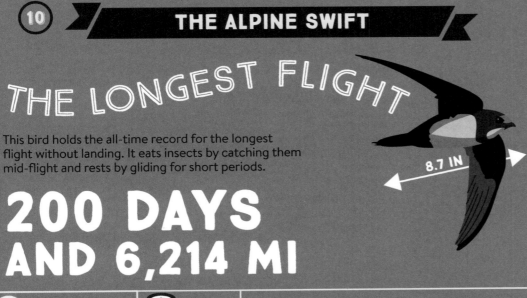

ELEPHANT 600 TO 660 DAYS (20 to 22 months)

GORILLA 250 TO 270 DAYS (8 to 9 months)

RABBIT 31 DAYS (1 month)

13 DAYS

UNITED STATES, CENTRAL AMERICA

1 TO 3 LITTERS A YEAR

8 BABIES PER LITTER ON AVERAGE (up to 20)

WEIGHT AND SIZE OF THE NEWBORNS: 0.005 OZ AND 0.591 IN (the size of a bee)

---

9 ## THE MAYFLY

THE SHORTEST LIFE SPAN

This insect holds the record for the shortest life span in the animal kingdom. Depending on the species, the mayfly's time on Earth varies from as little as a few minutes to a few days.

LESS THAN 5 MINUTES (the adult life span of the species *Dolania americana*)

THERE ARE MORE THAN 3,000 SPECIES OF MAYFLIES.

With just 5 minutes to live, the female has to find a partner, mate, and lay eggs.

MAYFLIES SPEND TWO YEARS AS LARVAE.

SOUTHERN UNITED STATES

THE PACIFIC OCEAN OCTOPUS

11 ### LONGEST INCUBATION PERIOD

The female octopus of the species *Graneledone boreopacifica* glues her eggs to a rock face and then crawls over them, guarding them and keeping them warm until they hatch.

FOUR AND A HALF YEARS

160 THE NUMBER OF EGGS INCUBATED

THE CEPHALOPOD WITH THE LONGEST LIFE SPAN

PACIFIC OCEAN

Right after hatching, the young octopuses fend for themselves, as they are capable of hunting small prey.

---

10 ## THE ALPINE SWIFT

THE LONGEST FLIGHT

This bird holds the all-time record for the longest flight without landing. It eats insects by catching them mid-flight and rests by gliding for short periods.

8.7 IN

200 DAYS AND 6,214 MI

SOUTHERN EUROPE AND AFRICA

2.8 TO 4.2 OZ

Scientists were able to study the swifts' flight during their winter migration from Europe to Africa thanks to data recorders that were attached to their backs.

---

12 ## CUVIER'S BEAKED WHALE

RECORD FOR HOLDING BREATH

This little beaked whale can hold its breath longer than any other mammal. To hunt, it dives incredibly deep beneath the sea while holding its breath.

DIVES 9,843 FT DEEP

TIME SPENT UNDER WATER WITHOUT BREATHING: 2 H 18 MIN (12 times longer than the human record)

ABOUT 20 TO 23 FT

RECOVERY TIME AT THE SURFACE: 2 MIN

5.5 TO 7.7 TONS

TEMPERATE AND TROPICAL SEAS

THE POSIDONIA MEADOWS

⑬

FROM 164 FT DEEP TO THE SURFACE

SLOW GROWTH: BETWEEN 2 AND 4 INCHES A YEAR

BETWEEN 80,000 AND 200,000 YEARS OLD

UP TO 9.3 MI LONG

THE OLDEST LIVING ORGANISM

NEEDS PROTECTING!

Its ability to produce oxygen and its role in promoting biodiversity make it a major environmental concern.

 **MEDITERRANEAN SEA**

These meadows are underwater prairies filled with plants that produce fruit and flowers. The oldest of them is found off the coast of Formentera, a Spanish island.

---

⑭ THE VIRGINIA SPIDERWORT

THE FLOWER WITH THE THE SHORTEST LIFE

24 IN

The Virgina Spiderwort is one of the shortest-lived flowers in the world. The "wort" part of its name comes from the Old English word "wyrt," which means "plant" or "herb."

12 HOURS
The flower opens in the morning and dies at night, on the same day.

EXISTS IN 3 COLORS

🇺🇸 **VIRGINIA UNITED STATES**

AROUND 60 SPECIES OF SPIDERWORT

THE PITON DE LA FOURNAISE

THE LONGEST ERUPTION

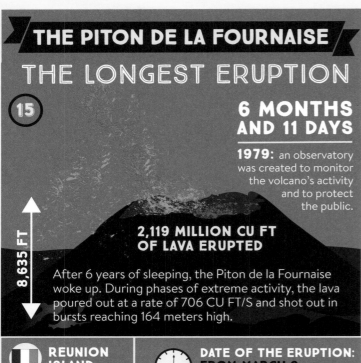

⑮

6 MONTHS AND 11 DAYS

1979: an observatory was created to monitor the volcano's activity and to protect the public.

2,119 MILLION CU FT OF LAVA ERUPTED

8,635 FT

After 6 years of sleeping, the Piton de la Fournaise woke up. During phases of extreme activity, the lava poured out at a rate of 706 CU FT/S and shot out in bursts reaching 164 meters high.

🇫🇷 **REUNION ISLAND FRANCE**

🕐 **DATE OF THE ERUPTION: FROM MARCH 9– SEPTEMBER 20, 1998**

---

⑯ THE SCHÖNBRUNN ZOO

THE OLDEST ZOO

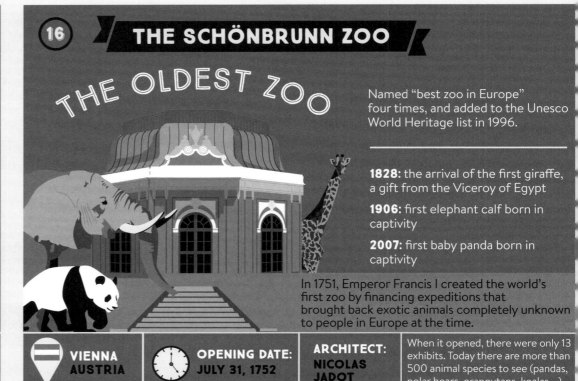

Named "best zoo in Europe" four times, and added to the Unesco World Heritage list in 1996.

1828: the arrival of the first giraffe, a gift from the Viceroy of Egypt

1906: first elephant calf born in captivity

2007: first baby panda born in captivity

In 1751, Emperor Francis I created the world's first zoo by financing expeditions that brought back exotic animals completely unknown to people in Europe at the time.

🇦🇹 **VIENNA AUSTRIA**

🕐 **OPENING DATE: JULY 31, 1752**

ARCHITECT: NICOLAS JADOT

When it opened, there were only 13 exhibits. Today there are more than 500 animal species to see (pandas, polar bears, orangutans, koalas ...).

---

⑰ THE GREAT WALL OF CHINA

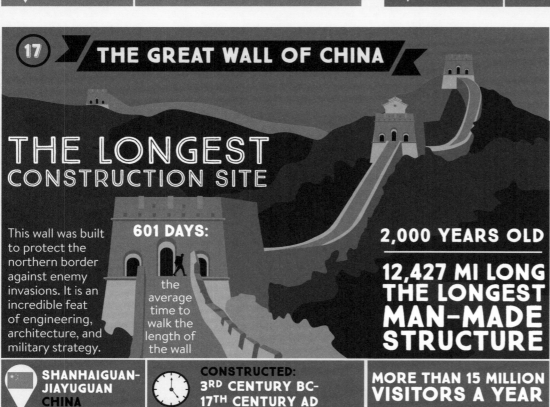

THE LONGEST CONSTRUCTION SITE

This wall was built to protect the northern border against enemy invasions. It is an incredible feat of engineering, architecture, and military strategy.

601 DAYS: the average time to walk the length of the wall

2,000 YEARS OLD

12,427 MI LONG THE LONGEST MAN-MADE STRUCTURE

🇨🇳 **SHANHAIGUAN-JIAYUGUAN CHINA**

🕐 **CONSTRUCTED: 3RD CENTURY BC-17TH CENTURY AD**

MORE THAN 15 MILLION VISITORS A YEAR

---

⑱ THE EDEN THEATER

THE OLDEST CINEMA IN THE WORLD
Located in a small town in the South of France, it was named a historical monument in 1996.

SEPTEMBER 21, 1895: the first public screening of the Lumière brothers' films

21 MARCH, 1899: the first priced cinema screening

2013: reopens after being restored to its original state, only equipped with modern technology

🇫🇷 **LA CIOTAT FRANCE**

🕐 **OPENED: JUNE 15, 1889**

166 SEATS

THE LONDON UNDERGROUND

19

ITS NICKNAME: "THE TUBE," OR "THE UNDERGROUND"

BEGAN SERVICE ON: JANUARY 10, 1863 AT PADDINGTON STATION

CONSTRUCTION: **3 YEARS** (1860-1863)

LONDON UNITED KINGOM

THE OLDEST METRO SYSTEM IN THE WORLD

To construct it, engineers made use of the most advanced railway construction technologies available at the time. It was an enormous amount of work digging those underground tunnels!

1890: steam-powered trains were replaced with the first electric train cars.

---

21 GN-Z11

THE OLDEST KNOWN GALAXY

13.4 BILLION YEARS OLD (400 million years after the Big Bang)

For comparison, the universe is estimated to be 13.8 billion years old, and the Earth 4.5 billion years old.

Spotted by the Hubble and Spitzer space telescopes, the GN-z11 galaxy is the oldest galaxy ever discovered. It is also the farthest ever observed.

25 TIMES SMALLER THAN THE MILKY WAY

 URSA MAJOR CONSTELLATION

---

20 GENNADY PADALKA

THE LONGEST TIME SPENT IN SPACE

878 DAYS 11 H 31 MIN (total combined time)

5 MISSIONS BETWEEN 1998 AND 2015

Because the human body is not designed for weightlessness, trips to space can only last so long. Gennady is currently the person who has spent the most time in space.

2 HOURS OF EXERCISE PER DAY to counteract the muscle and bone deterioration caused by weightlessness, and to maintain a well-functioning cardiovascular system.

2-3 DAYS: the amount of time it takes to adapt to zero gravity.

RUSSIA

---

22 BRANKO PETROVIĆ

THE MEN'S APNEA RECORD

11 MIN 54 SEC UNDERWATER WITHOUT BREATHING

Branko Petrović beat the world record for static apnea: a discipline that involves lying facedown and holding your breath underwater without moving. It is practiced in pairs for safety reasons.

---

23 JOHN ISNER VS. NICOLAS MAHUT

THE LONGEST GAME OF TENNIS

LENGTH OF MATCH : 11 H 5 MIN, PLAYED OVER 3 DAYS

On June 22, 2010, at Wimbledon, players John Isner and Nicolas Mahut began a legendary tennis match: the longest in the history of the sport.
12 RECORDS: number of games (183), points played (980), aces (216), balls used (126), length of set (70-68) ...
16,000: THE AMOUNT OF CALORIES BURNT BY THE PLAYERS

JOHN ISNER

5 SETS
4-6
6-3
7-6
6-7
70-68

WINNER

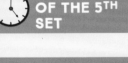 **8 H: LENGTH OF THE 5TH SET**

 LONDON UNITED KINGOM

 SERBIA — RECORD SET ON OCTOBER 7, 2014

---

24 NATALIA MOLCHANOVA

THE WOMEN'S APNEA RECORD

9 MIN 2 SEC UNDERWATER WITHOUT BREATHING (3 seconds longer than all the men participating in this competition)

This free-diving champion and former president of the Russian Free Dive Federation holds the women's world record for static apnea. She disappeared at sea in 2015.

41 WORLD RECORDS, INCLUDING 20 GOLD MEDALS

 RUSSIA

 RECORD SET ON JUNE 28, 2013

40 YEARS OLD: the age at which she started diving

---

25 MARTIN STREL

LONG SWIM RECORD

SWAM A TOTAL OF 3,273 MI

People call him the "Fishman." In 2007, he swam the length of the Amazon River, the longest and most dangerous river in the world, braving snakes, piranhas, and crocodiles.

4 LONG-DISTANCE RECORDS

 MOKRONOG SLOVENIA

LOST 37 LB OVER THE COURSE OF THE ENDEAVOR

66 DAYS OF SWIMMING WITHOUT STOPPING = 10 HOURS A DAY

QUIETEST
LOUDEST

- DINOSAURS
- ANIMALS
- HUMANS
- ARCHITECTURE
- TECHNOLOGY
- ASTRONOMY
- NATURE
- SPORTS

Sound

The intensity of a sound corresponds to the amount of energy a sound wave emits. The stronger the intensity, the louder the sound. Sound is measured with a sound level meter and is calculated in decibels (dB), on a scale of 0 to 200 dB. But be careful—measuring in decibels is different than simple addition: every time you go up 10 decibels, the power of the sound multiples by 10.

85 DB	120 DB	190 DB
HAZARDOUS FOR HUMANS	THE SOUND CAUSES PAIN	THE SOUND CAN KILL A PERSON

THE QUIETEST	THE LOUDEST

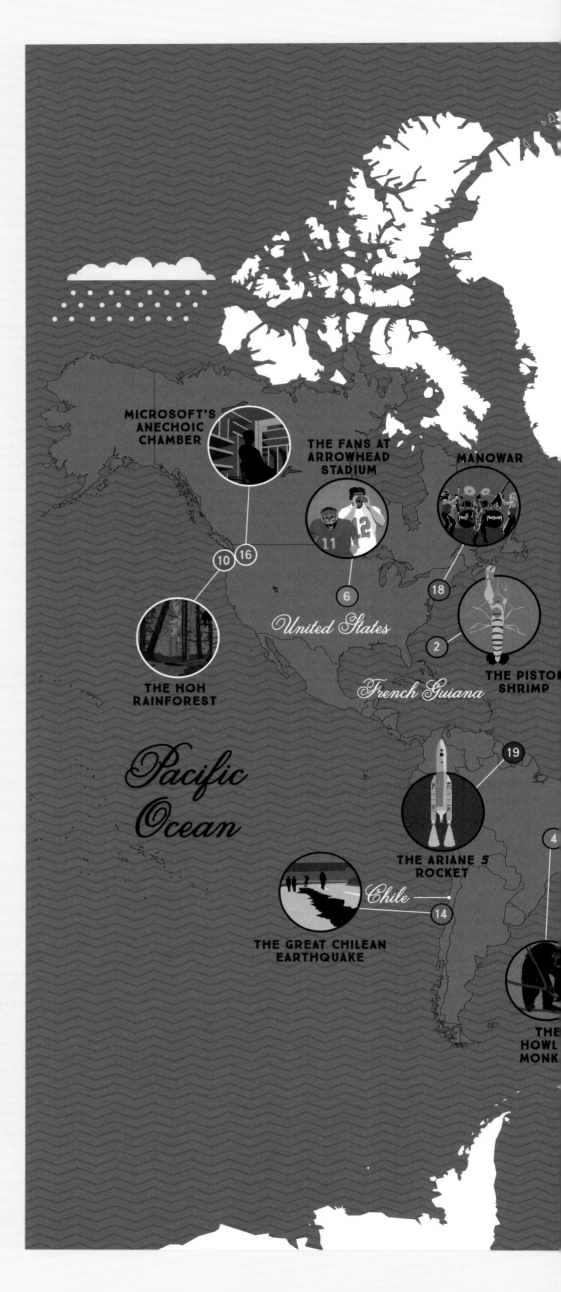

MICROSOFT'S ANECHOIC CHAMBER

THE FANS AT ARROWHEAD STADIUM

MANOWAR

10 16

6

11

18

2

United States

French Guiana

THE PISTOL SHRIMP

THE HOH RAINFOREST

Pacific Ocean

19

THE ARIANE 5 ROCKET

Chile

14

4

THE GREAT CHILEAN EARTHQUAKE

THE HOWLER MONKEY

THE AIR CANNON

15

THE WATER BOATMAN

THE EUROPEAN TREE FROG

5

3

France

8

THE FORMULA 1 RACE

13

SINGING SANDS

Sahara Desert

THE ROTORFLY

17

Russia

20

THE TUNGUSKA METEOROID

THE ERUPTION OF MOUNT TAMBORA

11

Indonesia

NEVILLE SHARP

9

Australia

Indian Ocean

THE VUVUZELA

7

South Africa

Atlantic Ocean

THE SPERM WHALE

1

ICEBERG CALVING

12

Antarctica

QUIETEST

LOUDEST

1 THE SPERM WHALE

THE LOUDEST MAMMAL
UP TO 65.6 FT

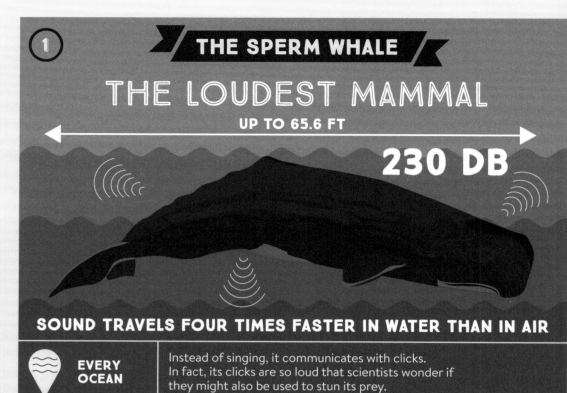

230 DB

SOUND TRAVELS FOUR TIMES FASTER IN WATER THAN IN AIR

EVERY OCEAN

Instead of singing, it communicates with clicks. In fact, its clicks are so loud that scientists wonder if they might also be used to stun its prey.

2 THE PISTOL SHRIMP

THE LOUDEST CRUSTACEAN

218 DB

= 9 times louder than a symphony orchestra

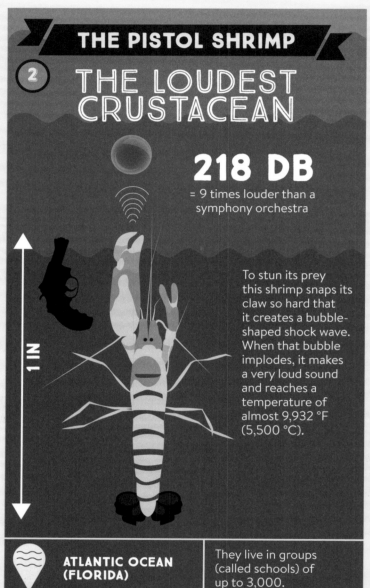

1 IN

To stun its prey this shrimp snaps its claw so hard that it creates a bubble-shaped shock wave. When that bubble implodes, it makes a very loud sound and reaches a temperature of almost 9,932 °F (5,500 °C).

ATLANTIC OCEAN (FLORIDA)

They live in groups (called schools) of up to 3,000.

3 THE EUROPEAN TREE FROG

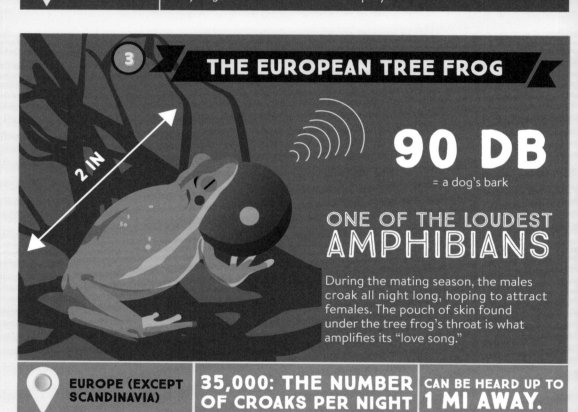

2 IN

90 DB

= a dog's bark

ONE OF THE LOUDEST AMPHIBIANS

During the mating season, the males croak all night long, hoping to attract females. The pouch of skin found under the tree frog's throat is what amplifies its "love song."

EUROPE (EXCEPT SCANDINAVIA)

35,000: THE NUMBER OF CROAKS PER NIGHT

CAN BE HEARD UP TO 1 MI AWAY.

4 THE HOWLER MONKEY

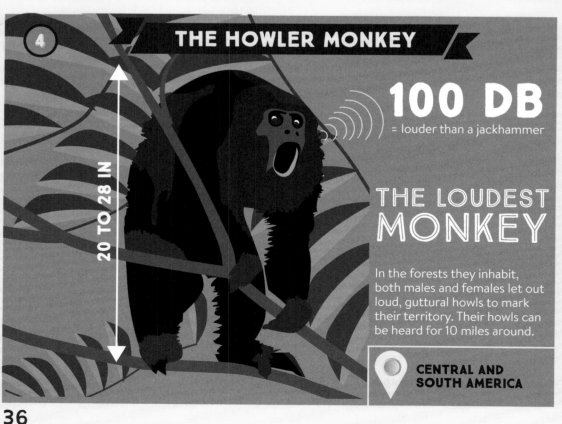

20 TO 28 IN

100 DB

= louder than a jackhammer

THE LOUDEST MONKEY

In the forests they inhabit, both males and females let out loud, guttural howls to mark their territory. Their howls can be heard for 10 miles around.

CENTRAL AND SOUTH AMERICA

5 THE WATER BOATMAN

THE LOUDEST INSECT

99 DB

= as loud as a motorcycle

The male produces a loud chirp by rubbing its private parts against its belly in the hope of attracting females. Compared to its size, this insect produces the loudest sound in the animal kingdom. Luckily, 99% of it is absorbed by water.

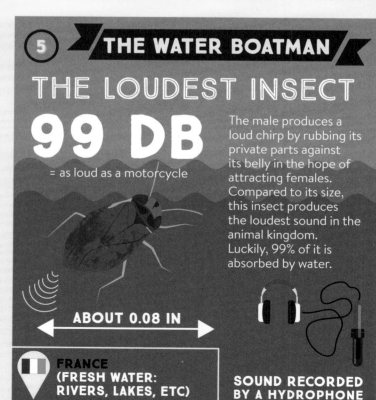

ABOUT 0.08 IN

FRANCE (FRESH WATER: RIVERS, LAKES, ETC)

SOUND RECORDED BY A HYDROPHONE

6 THE FANS AT ARROWHEAD STADIUM

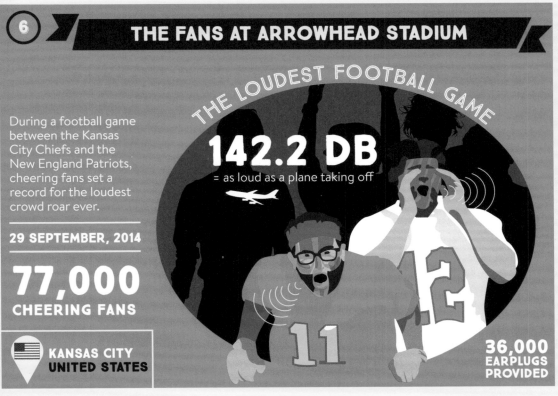

During a football game between the Kansas City Chiefs and the New England Patriots, cheering fans set a record for the loudest crowd roar ever.

29 SEPTEMBER, 2014

77,000
CHEERING FANS

THE LOUDEST FOOTBALL GAME

142.2 DB
= as loud as a plane taking off

36,000 EARPLUGS PROVIDED

📍 **KANSAS CITY**
UNITED STATES

7 THE VUVUZELA

THE LOUDEST INSTRUMENT

This plastic horn first appeared in the 60s and has been used by cheering soccer fans ever since. It is also used as a musical instrument.

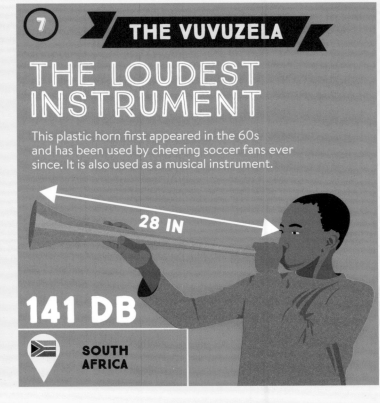

28 IN

141 DB

📍 **SOUTH AFRICA**

9 NEVILLE SHARP

RECORD FOR LOUDEST BURP

110.6 DB
= the sound level in a nightclub

Burping is the sound of air being pushed out of the stomach and through the mouth. Although everyone burps, the sound they make varies in volume.

📍 **AUSTRALIA**

HIS TRICK: DRINK 20 OZ OF CARBONATED BEVERAGES

8 THE FORMULA 1 RACE

95 DB
IN THE COMMENTATOR'S BOOTH

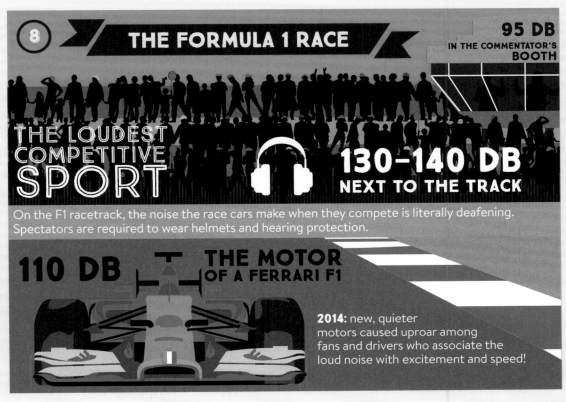

THE LOUDEST COMPETITIVE SPORT

🎧 **130-140 DB**
NEXT TO THE TRACK

On the F1 racetrack, the noise the race cars make when they compete is literally deafening. Spectators are required to wear helmets and hearing protection.

110 DB
THE MOTOR OF A FERRARI F1

2014: new, quieter motors caused uproar among fans and drivers who associate the loud noise with excitement and speed!

10 THE HOH RAINFOREST

A SANCTUARY FOR SILENCE

Even in nature, it is hard to find places that are completely free of man-made noise. So, in 2005, the acoustic ecologist Gordon Hempton created a sanctuary for silence to protect the rainforest from noise pollution.

30 TO 40 DB

NO PLANES, TRUCKS, OR CARS CAN ENTER THE PROTECTED ZONE.

THE SANCTUARY'S NAME: "ONE SQUARE INCH OF SILENCE"

 OLYMPIC NATIONAL PARK
UNITED STATES

 NAMED UNESCO SITE IN 1981

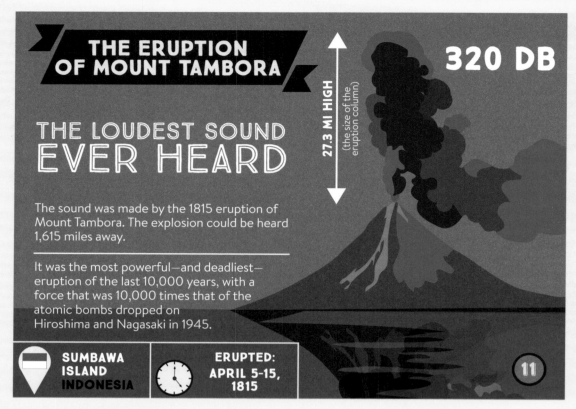

THE ERUPTION OF MOUNT TAMBORA

THE LOUDEST SOUND EVER HEARD

27.3 MI HIGH (the size of the eruption column)

320 DB

The sound was made by the 1815 eruption of Mount Tambora. The explosion could be heard 1,615 miles away.

It was the most powerful—and deadliest—eruption of the last 10,000 years, with a force that was 10,000 times that of the atomic bombs dropped on Hiroshima and Nagasaki in 1945.

SUMBAWA ISLAND INDONESIA

ERUPTED: APRIL 5-15, 1815

11

ICEBERG CALVING

12

ONE OF THE LOUDEST SOUNDS IN NATURE

When huge chunks of ice break off of a glacier (a process called calving), it makes an enormous cracking sound. Scientists named this sound "the bloop", and it can be heard underwater up to 3,107 miles away.

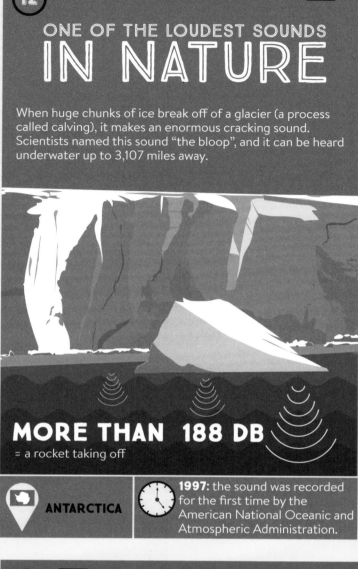

MORE THAN 188 DB
= a rocket taking off

ANTARCTICA

1997: the sound was recorded for the first time by the American National Oceanic and Atmospheric Administration.

13

SINGING SANDS

THE LOUDEST DESERTS

110 DB
= an electric saw

THE SOUND TRAVELS 6.2 MI

Singing sands are found in nearly 30 deserts throughout the world.

SAHARA DESERT AFRICA

This phenomenon occurs in sandy deserts: when grains of sand detach from the dunes, the avalanche produces a deep, droning hum that sounds like a mix between a deep roar and a tuba.

14

THE GREAT CHILEAN EARTHQUAKE

THE BIGGEST EARTHQUAKE

The earthquake hit Valdivia, Chile, on May 22, 1960: it had a magnitude of 9.5 on the Richter scale.

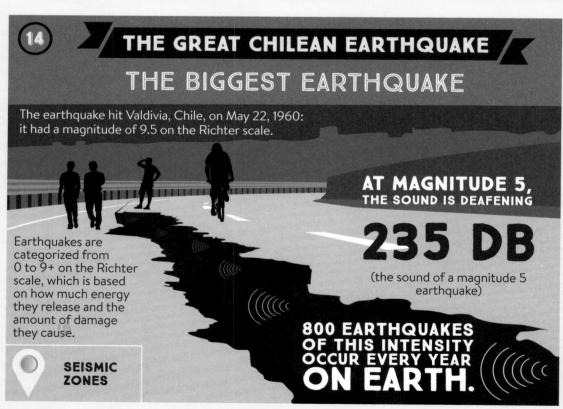

AT MAGNITUDE 5, THE SOUND IS DEAFENING

235 DB

(the sound of a magnitude 5 earthquake)

Earthquakes are categorized from 0 to 9+ on the Richter scale, which is based on how much energy they release and the amount of damage they cause.

SEISMIC ZONES

800 EARTHQUAKES OF THIS INTENSITY OCCUR EVERY YEAR ON EARTH.

15

THE AIR CANNON

ONE OF THE LOUDEST MACHINES

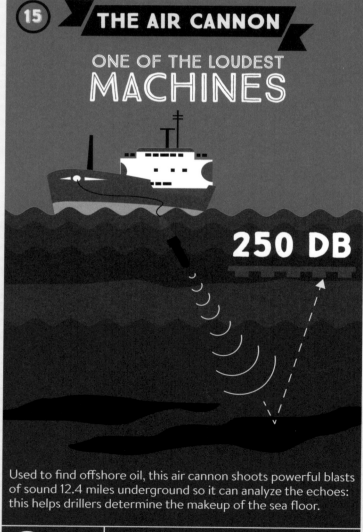

250 DB

Used to find offshore oil, this air cannon shoots powerful blasts of sound 12.4 miles underground so it can analyze the echoes: this helps drillers determine the makeup of the sea floor.

RUSSIA

621 MI: THE DISTANCE
THE SOUND TRAVELS UNDERWATER

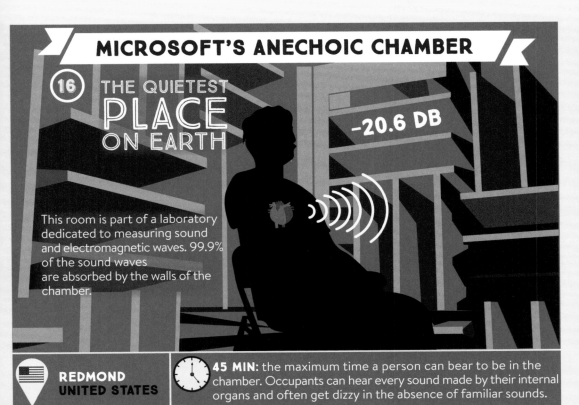

MICROSOFT'S ANECHOIC CHAMBER

16 THE QUIETEST **PLACE** ON EARTH

−20.6 DB

This room is part of a laboratory dedicated to measuring sound and electromagnetic waves. 99.9% of the sound waves are absorbed by the walls of the chamber.

 REDMOND UNITED STATES

45 MIN: the maximum time a person can bear to be in the chamber. Occupants can hear every sound made by their internal organs and often get dizzy in the absence of familiar sounds.

17 THE ROTORFLY

THE QUIETEST HELICOPTER

70 DB

(as loud as a vacuum cleaner)

RUSSIA

With a range of 217 miles, it can fly at a max altitude of 13,123 feet and carry up to 573 pounds.

THE WORLD'S LOUDEST BAND

Manowar is a heavy metal band known for its extra-loud music.

 **NEW YORK UNITED STATES**   **CONCERT ON JULY 9, 2008, IN GERMANY**

18 **MANOWAR**

139 DB

the noise level during the song **"CALL TO ARMS"**

THE ARIANE 5 ROCKET

THE LOUDEST TAKEOFF

Ariane 5 was built by several European nations for the purpose of sending satellites into space and placing them into orbit. The rocket gets its thrust from Vulcain 2 rocket engines, which are as powerful as 2 high-speed trains!

190 DB

during takeoff

174 FT HIGH

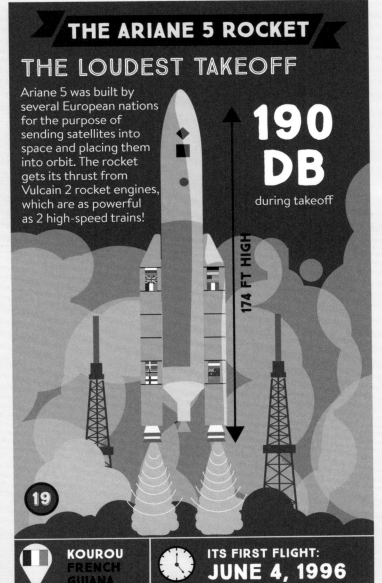

19

 KOUROU FRENCH GUIANA   **ITS FIRST FLIGHT: JUNE 4, 1996**

20 THE TUNGUSKA METEOROID

ONE OF THE MOST POWERFUL EXPLOSIONS

310 DB

(the equivalent of 250 nuclear bombs)

Scientists suspect that an asteroid measuring 33 feet wide exploded 16,404 feet above ground, producing a giant fireball while burning up in the atmosphere.

 RUSSIA TUNGUSKA REGION   **JUNE 30, 1908**   **49,421 ACRES OF BURNT VEGETATION AND 60 MILLION TREES DESTROYED**

COLDEST
HOTTEST

- DINOSAURS
- ANIMALS
- HUMANS
- ARCHITECTURE

- TECHNOLOGY
- ASTRONOMY
- NATURE
- SPORTS

Temperature

Since its invention in the seventeenth century, the thermometer has been one of the main instruments for measuring temperatures. In the United States and a few other countries, people measure temperature in degrees Fahrenheit, while the rest of the world uses degrees Celsius. To understand each other better, all scientists use the same unit of measure: they calculate temperature in Kelvin.

1 K (KELVIN) = − 272.15 °C (DEGREES CELSIUS)	1 K = − 475 °F (DEGREES FAHRENHEIT)

THE COLDEST	THE HOTTEST

Alaska

10

THE WOOD
FROG

Canada

8

THE ARCTIC
GROUND SQUIRREL

7

United States

FURNACE
CREEK

*Pacific
Ocean*

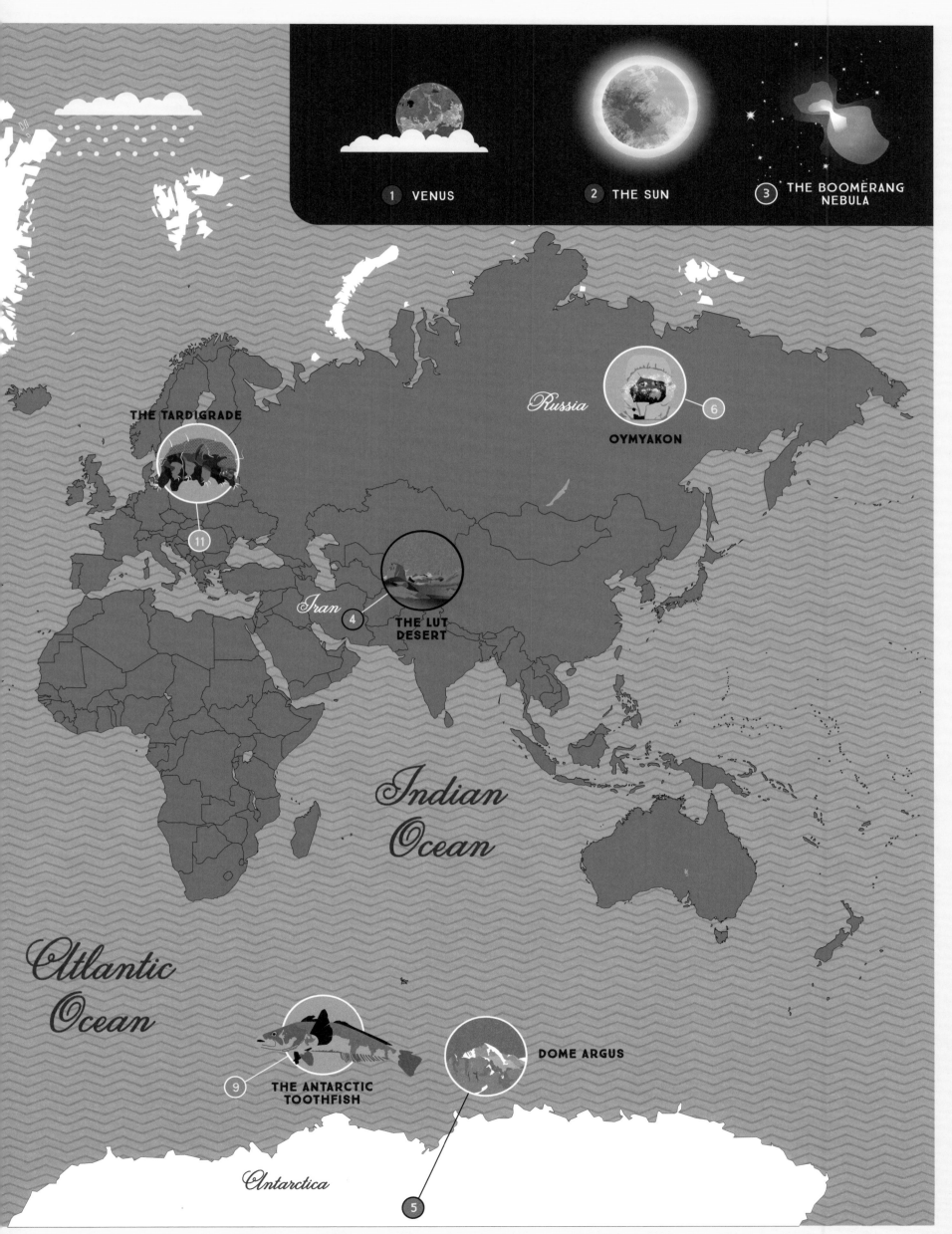

COLDEST ○ HOTTEST

1 VENUS

THE HOTTEST PLANET IN OUR SOLAR SYSTEM

DISTANCE FROM THE SUN: 67 MILLION MI

878 °F
(470 °C)

compared with 59 °F (15 °C), the average temperature on Earth

Venus is the second-closest planet to the Sun. The thick clouds covering the planet block out 80% of the light while its greenhouse effect locks in the Sun's heat.

NICKNAMED THE MORNING STAR AND THE EVENING STAR.

 SOLAR SYSTEM

HEAT + UNBREATHABLE ATMOSPHERE = NO POSSIBILITY OF LIFE

2 THE SUN

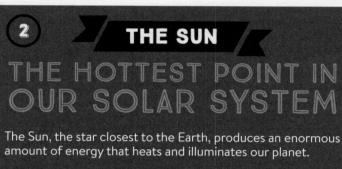

THE HOTTEST POINT IN OUR SOLAR SYSTEM

The Sun, the star closest to the Earth, produces an enormous amount of energy that heats and illuminates our planet.

TEMPERATURE OF THE SUN'S CORE:
27 MILLION °F
(15 million °C)

ITS DIAMETER:
864,938 MI
(110 times greater than Earth's diameter)

93 MILLION MI FROM EARTH

SURFACE TEMPERATURE:
9,932 °F
(5,500 °C)

A star's color lets us know how hot it is. A yellow star like the Sun has an average temperature of 9,932 °F.
Blue = twice as hot
Red = half as hot

 AGE: AROUND 4.6 BILLION YEARS OLD

OUR SUN HAS ALREADY LIVED HALF OF ITS LIFE.

SOLAR SYSTEM

4 THE LUT DESERT

THE HOTTEST PLACE ON EARTH
159.2 °F
(70.6 °C)

This hostile, uninhabited desert is a vast salty expanse, swept by violent winds.

IRAN | **GROUND TEMPERATURE MEASURED BY SATELLITE IN 2005.** | **THE LUT DESERT WAS INSCRIBED ON THE UNESCO WOLRD HERITAGE LIST IN 2016.**

3 THE BOOMERANG NEBULA

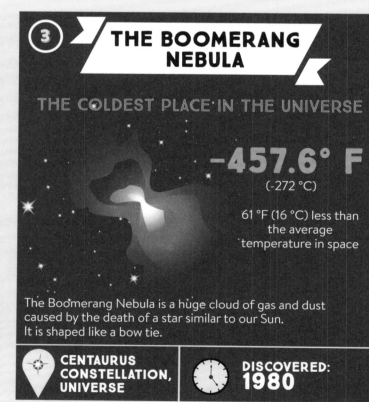

THE COLDEST PLACE IN THE UNIVERSE

−457.6° F
(−272 °C)

61 °F (16 °C) less than the average temperature in space

The Boomerang Nebula is a huge cloud of gas and dust caused by the death of a star similar to our Sun. It is shaped like a bow tie.

 CENTAURUS CONSTELLATION, UNIVERSE | **DISCOVERED: 1980**

5 DOME ARGUS

Dome Argus: 13,428 ft

ANTARCTICA

THE COLDEST PLACE

−135.7 °F
(−93.2 °C)
Four times colder than the inside of a freezer

The highest ice dome in Antarctica, Dome Argus is considered the coldest place on planet Earth.

HIGHEST POINT IN ANTARCTICA:
MOUNT VINSON
16,049 FT

 TEMPERATURE MEASURED BY THE SATELLITE LANDSAT 7 ON AUGUST 10, 2010.

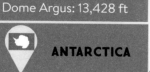

6

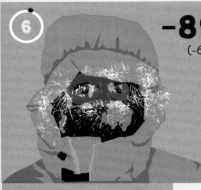

-89.9 °F
(-67.8 °C)

OYMYAKON

ONE OF THE
COLDEST VILLAGES

In this village of about 500, the ground is frozen nearly all year-round. Fruit and vegetables are impossible to grow and planes cannot even land here.

9 MONTHS OF WINTER

3 HOURS OF DAYLIGHT IN DECEMBER

 COLDEST TEMPERATURE ON RECORD TAKEN FEBRUARY 6, 1933.

 SIBERIA RUSSIA

98.6 °F (37 °C)
BODY TEMPERATURE DURING NORMAL WEATHER

LENGTH OF HIBERNATION:
 7 MONTHS

 CANADA

THE ARCTIC GROUND SQUIRREL

8 THE MAMMAL WITH
THE LOWEST
BODY TEMPERATURE

The Arctic ground squirrel hibernates all winter long. It is the only mammal whose body temperature drops below 32 °F (0 °C) without its blood freezing!

ARCTIC GROUND SQUIRREL

37 °F (2.8 °C)

MARMOT

41 °F (5 °C)

7

FURNACE CREEK

THE HOTTEST
INHABITED PLACE
134.1 °F
(56.7 °C)

The town of Furnace Creek (population: less than 20) is located in Death Valley. Its desert climate means there is practically no rain all year long.

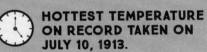 **CALIFORNIA UNITED STATES**

HOTTEST TEMPERATURE ON RECORD TAKEN ON JULY 10, 1913.

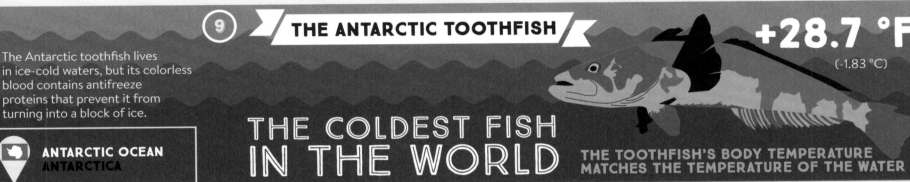

9 THE ANTARCTIC TOOTHFISH

The Antarctic toothfish lives in ice-cold waters, but its colorless blood contains antifreeze proteins that prevent it from turning into a block of ice.

ANTARCTIC OCEAN ANTARCTICA

+28.7 °F (-1.83 °C)

THE COLDEST FISH
IN THE WORLD

THE TOOTHFISH'S BODY TEMPERATURE MATCHES THE TEMPERATURE OF THE WATER

---

10 THE WOOD FROG

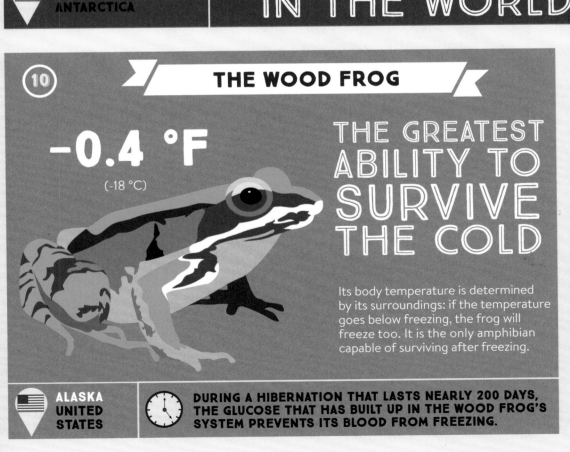

-0.4 °F
(-18 °C)

THE GREATEST
ABILITY TO
SURVIVE
THE COLD

Its body temperature is determined by its surroundings: if the temperature goes below freezing, the frog will freeze too. It is the only amphibian capable of surviving after freezing.

ALASKA UNITED STATES

DURING A HIBERNATION THAT LASTS NEARLY 200 DAYS, THE GLUCOSE THAT HAS BUILT UP IN THE WOOD FROG'S SYSTEM PREVENTS ITS BLOOD FROM FREEZING.

---

11 THE TARDIGRADE

RECORD ABILITY TO WITHSTAND
HOT AND COLD

+302 °F (+150 °C)
The maximum temperature it can withstand: it can survive temperatures higher than boiling water.

-454 °F (-270 °C)
Tardigrades sent into space in 2007 survived the extreme cold of the universe.

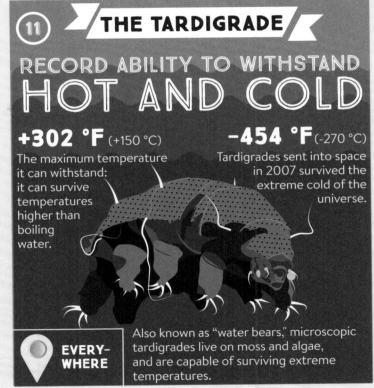

EVERY-WHERE

Also known as "water bears," microscopic tardigrades live on moss and algae, and are capable of surviving extreme temperatures.

·INDEX·

Recordmania: Atlas of the Incredible

Text by Emmanuelle Figueras
Illustrations by Alexandre Verhille and Sarah Tavernier

Translated from French by Kevin St. John

Published by Little Gestalten, Berlin 2018
ISBN: 978-3-89955-814-2

The German edition is available under ISBN 978-3-89955-813-5.

Proofreading by Benjamin Barlow
Printed by Printer Trento, Italy
Made in Europe

The French original edition *Recordmania Cartographie de L'Incroyable*
was published by Éditions Milan. © for the French original:
Éditions Milan, 2017. © for the English edition: Little Gestalten,
an imprint of Die Gestalten Verlag GmbH & Co. KG, Berlin 2018.

For more information, please visit little.gestalten.com.

Bibliographic information published by the Deutsche Nationalbibliothek:
The Deutsche Nationalbibliothek lists this publication in the
Deutsche Nationalbibliografie; detailed bibliographic data are available
online at www.dnb.de.

This book was printed on paper certified according to the standards
of the FSC®.

MIX
Paper from
responsible sources
FSC
www.fsc.org
FSC® C015829

Recordmania: Atlas of the Incredible

Text by Emmanuelle Figueras
Illustrations by Alexandre Verhille and Sarah Tavernier

Translated from French by Kevin St. John

Published by Little Gestalten, Berlin 2018
ISBN: 978-3-89955-814-2

The German edition is available under ISBN 978-3-89955-813-5.

Proofreading by Benjamin Barlow
Printed by Printer Trento, Italy
Made in Europe

The French original edition *Recordmania Cartographie de L'Incroyable*
was published by Éditions Milan. © for the French original:
Éditions Milan, 2017. © for the English edition: Little Gestalten,
an imprint of Die Gestalten Verlag GmbH & Co. KG, Berlin 2018.

For more information, please visit little.gestalten.com.

Bibliographic information published by the Deutsche Nationalbibliothek:
The Deutsche Nationalbibliothek lists this publication in the
Deutsche Nationalbibliografie; detailed bibliographic data are available
online at www.dnb.de.

This book was printed on paper certified according to the standards
of the FSC®.

FSC
www.fsc.org
MIX
Paper from
responsible sources
FSC® C015829